# MOM EGG REVIEW

## 2016  VOL. 14

### "Change"

Half-Shell Press
New York

*Mom Egg Review* is an annual collection of poetry, fiction, creative prose, and art by and about mothers and motherhood. *MER* promotes and celebrates the creative force of mother artists and sustains community through publications, performances, workshops, and online at www.momeggreview.com.

www.momeggreview.com
www.facebook.com/themomegg
Twitter: @themomegg
Contact:  themomegg@gmail.com

Front Cover Image: "Happy Breastfish" by Sally Deskins.

"Ars Poetica" by Hilde Weisert was originally published in *The Scheme of Things*, 2015, David Robert Books, Cincinnati, Ohio.

*Mom Egg Review* is a member of the Community of Literary Magazines and Presses.

This publication has been made possible, in part, by a grants program of the New York State Council on the Arts, a state arts agency, and the Community of Literary Magazines and Presses. *Mom Egg Review* is grateful for this generous support. *Mom Egg Review* is also grateful for the assistance of The Motherhood Foundation, and for the support of individual donors.  With thanks to founding editor Alana Ruben Free and founding publishers, Joy Rose & Mamapalooza.

ISBN-13: 978-0-9915107-2-6     (Half-Shell Press)
ISBN-10: 0991510720

Mom Egg Review
Half-Shell Press
PO Box 9037
Bardonia, NY 10954
info@themomegg.com

# MOM EGG REVIEW
# 2016 VOL. 14

# "Change"

Editor-in-Chief
Marjorie Tesser

Poetry Editor
Jennifer Jean

Readers for Vol. 14
Jessie Bacho
Patrice Boyer Claeys
Elizabeth Lara
Jennifer Martelli
Ana C.H. Silva
Becky Tipper
Cindy Veach
Nancy Vona
Paulette Warren

# EDITORS' NOTES

Marjorie Tesser
Editor-in-Chief

Welcome to Mom Egg Review Vol. 14! This issue explores "Change."

Change can be a lightning bolt, a bud's unfurling, or the inexorable melt of ice caps. A body swells with pregnancy, bends with illness, shrinks with age; a couple evolves or severs; a child slowly cycles through a myriad of incarnations. Or tornado, bomb, gunshot.

Change is acute and cyclical, rhythmic and cataclysmic, personal and political, abstract and physical, natural and un-, absolute and incremental, often too gradual or too precipitous.

Change is not just one-directional flow, something that happens to us; we can affect its course, embrace, finesse, challenge, or stem it. Mothers often serve as society's first responders and interlocutors of change for children and, often, others. There is also change that we make. Mothers effect change by example and by action, by our works—life and art.

The works in this issue look unblinkingly at change; they investigate, interrogate, and even implement change, local and global. Enjoy the frank, thoughtful, and powerful poems and stories in this issue. May they inspire you to create the good changes needed in your world.

Jennifer Jean
Poetry Editor

Life is comprised of a sequence of changes. We invite, confront, digest, resist, await, preempt, and surrender to change. We sleepwalk through change. "So I turned myself to face me/ But I've never caught a glimpse." That's from David Bowie about what happens when we don't "face the strange" of "Ch-ch-changes." We disconnect. Today, Bowie died. And, one friend admitted to me that her daylong anguish had as much to do with the loss of an iconic artist as with realizing that she too will face death—the ultimate change for each of us. Into ashes and dust. Her sharing this reckoning, her encapsulating it, staved off its pressure, lightened its weight, she said. That's what these current batch of *MER* poems do. These poems are Mason jars, each capturing a Change—not stopping its motion but isolating it for our notice. The Change flutters while we look on. Then we undo the jar top, and it's on its way. Like a child off to school, off to love, off to danger. A mother's relationship to change is particular—we must be attuned to it because what works in one stage of life doesn't work in another. We watch our bodies morph, our children's bodies evolve. We watch our own mothers diminish— golden goddesses who once ruled our world. Keepers of time, of love, of how-to, and no. No wonder the moon is a cross-cultural symbol of motherhood. We perceive her cyclicality. She's a seeming lady Lazarus. Really, the moon always is as it ever was. Solid rock. Like mother-love. Some things must change, but don't—some of our writers call out a striking example: that boa constrictor, Racism. Some changes are unnatural and must be resisted—such as the destruction of our environment. This issue of *Mom Egg Review* addresses these concerns, and more. I know you'll enjoy our writers' wonderful work as much as I did. I'm certain you'll lift your eyes from these pages and, like me, be: changed.

# CONTENTS

*Spring*

| | | |
|---|---|---|
| Amy Sawyer | 1 | PREGNANT JESUS |
| Deb Casey | 2 | NOTE TO THE RESTLESS ROVER WITHIN |
| Cindy Frenkel | 3 | SURRENDER AND ARRIVAL |
| Nadia Colburn | 4 | THE PHYSICAL WORLD |
| L.J. Sysko | 5 | SITZ BATH |
| Meghan Smith | 6 | THE FIRST FOUR WEEKS |
| Sarah Ghoshal | 7 | IT ALL HAPPENED SO FAST |
| Laura Sloan Patterson | 8 | THE GIRAFFE |
| Kassie Rubico | 8 | THE WAITING GAME    *Creative Prose* |
| Wendy Mnookin | 10 | CONSTELLATIONS |
| Sarah Evans | 11 | WINDOW    *Creative Prose* |
| Lisa Badner | 12 | WATCHING ADOPTION VIDEO WITH MY 8 YEAR OLD |
| Laura A. Ciraolo | 13 | THE USE OF ALL THINGS |
| Jenifer DeBellis | 14 | THE DETROIT INSTITUTE OF ARTS |
| Andrea Potos | 16 | DAUGHTER PEARL |
| Maura Snell | 16 | LEARNING |
| Joanne Esser | 17 | HIKE TO RATTLESNAKE LEDGE |
| Susan Vespoli | 18 | SONOGRAM |
| Sarah W. Bartlett | 19 | GENERATIONS |

*Summer*

| | | |
|---|---|---|
| Robyn Art | 20 | WHAT I ASSUMED ABOUT THE AFTERLIFE |
| Margo Berdeshevsky | 21 | HOW WE DARE NOT SEE    *Photograph* |
| Marian Kaplun Shapiro | 22 | DIVIDING LINE |
| Juanita Kirton | 23 | FATHER'S DAY |
| E.J. Antonio | 25 | SCRAPE |
| Elisabeth Weiss | 26 | CITY OF PROMISE |
| Ann Fisher-Wirth | 27 | IN THAT KITCHEN (SHE SPEAKS TO HERSELF) |
| Margaret Rapp | 28 | I SEE YOU |
| J.P. Howard | 29 | BLACK LIVES MATTER: A MAMA'S PERSPECTIVE    *Essay* |
| Emily R. Blumenfeld | 30 | A SUMMER TRUTH TELLING |
| Kelly Dolejsi | 31 | PERSEID, OR THE FIRST DAY OF SCHOOL |
| Charlotte Mandel | 32 | TYPHOON HAIYAN |
| Barbara Crooker | 33 | GLOBAL CLIMATE CHANGE |
| Puma Perl | 34 | HOLIDAY INN |
| Eve Packer | 35 | CARDS AND CURIOSITIES |
| Margo Berdeshevsky | 36 | DAILY BREAD |
| Margaret Rozga | 37 | THREE WOMEN SHARE TWO SANDWICHES    *Creative Prose* |
| Fay Chiang | 38 | CHANGE    *Creative Prose* |
| Robyn Art | 40 | FURTHER QUESTIONS ABOUT THE AFTERLIFE |
| Christine Stewart-Nunez | 41 | AGAINST MELANCHOLY (AS HILDEGARD DEFINES IT) |
| Megan Wynne | 42 | ABOUT TO BURST/COMPLETELY DRAINED    *Photograph* |

*Autumn*

| | | |
|---|---|---|
| Gwen North Reiss | 44 | SEPTEMBER AFTERNOON |
| Hilde Weisert | 45 | ARS POETICA |
| Tess Barry | 46 | BIRTH RE-ORDER |
| Carol Dorf | 46 | ADA |
| Ana C.H. Silva | 47 | HALTER TOP |
| Kelli Stevens Kane | 48 | STARLIGHT |
| Cindy Veach | 49 | ON THE GRAIN |
| John Wojtowicz | 51 | GROWING UP |
| Ann E. Michael | 52 | BICENTENNIAL SUMMER |
| Alison Condie Jaenicke | 54 | RED STRING OF FATE |
| Nadia Colburn | 55 | SHAPE |
| Jessica Martinez | 57 | TRANSITIONS |
| Jennifer Brooke | 59 | BLENDED FAMILY |
| Kate Falvey | 60 | GINGERBREAD MIX |
| Kimberly Weikert | 61 | LABOR PAINS |
| Donna Katzin | 62 | THE BUILDER |
| Felice Aull | 63 | DIVESTITURE |
| Carol Levin | 64 | NOW THAT THE NEST IS EMPTY |
| Katherine Durham Oldmixon | 65 | POST HASTE |
| Judith Waller Carroll | 65 | EMPTY NEST |
| Sandra Kohler | 66 | ASSAYING |
| Patrice Boyer Claeys | 67 | MOTHER'S TRIP TO RED LOBSTER |
| Deborah Batterman | 68 | A BRAIDED TALE   *Fiction* |
| Sarah Kennedy | 70 | OCCUPYING MOTHERHOOD   *Creative Prose* |
| Therese Gilardi | 71 | CHANGE OF LIVES   *Creative Prose* |
| Tsaurah Litzky | 73 | THE COCKTAIL DRESS   *Creative Prose* |
| Lorraine Currelley | 74 | TANGO   *Fiction* |
| Nancy Gerber | 76 | UNPACKING   *Creative Prose* |
| Heather Haldeman | 77 | MOVING ON   *Creative Prose* |
| Marion Cohen | 79 | THE NURSING TODDLER LEARNS ABOUT LIFE |
| Pam Bernard | 80 | THE GIFT   *Creative Prose* |

*Winter*

| | | |
|---|---|---|
| Zara Raab | 82 | WINTER CALENDARS |
| Kelli Russell Agodon | 83 | SONG OF THE QUIET VISITOR |
| Angelique Johnston | 84 | WALLPAPER CARS |
| Melissa Knox | 85 | MISCARRIAGE AT TEN WEEKS |
| Cathie Sandstrom | 85 | NO VOYAGING |
| Martha Silano | 86 | THE HARDEST PART ABOUT MOVING |
| Owen Lewis | 87 | URGENCY |
| Amy Pence | 88 | BIRTHDAY MONTH |
| Tracy Mishkin | 89 | CLINICAL TRIAL |
| Lisa Marie Brodsky | 90 | HYSTERECTOMY OF THE ROARING WOMAN |
| Brett Foster | 91 | MY MOTHER AS INADVERTENT OPTIMIST |
| Wendy Vardaman | 92 | #12 |
| Carley Moore | 93 | CODE |

Rachel Edmonds            94      LEAVING
Jamie Stern              95      DIDN'T WE JUST
Theta Pavis              96      FORM IN BLUE
M. Joy Rose              96      CHANGE
Jennifer Martelli        97      DROWNED GIRL AND DOOMED BOY
Lori Lamothe             98      THE AGORAPHOBIC'S DREAM
Carla Carlson            99      EXPANSION
Lois Marie Harrod        100     HUMMING TOO
Maria Brandt             101     WHATEVER WAS ALIVE    *Fiction*
Dana Bowman              102     DERAILMENT
Patricia Brody           103     RIGHT TO CHOOSE
Lori Lamothe             104     ON THE ROAD
Claudia Van Gerven       105     COURAGE
Wendy Vardaman           106     #24, #25

CONTRIBUTORS' NOTES 108

Amy Sawyer

## PREGNANT JESUS

You created the world by tossing stars
out of a burlap sack, You mixed the oceans
with an oversized whisk, sweating from
the labor of creation.  When the plan
went to hell, You zipped up a man's body
around that godly, feminine soul.
During those human years, You held life
in Your belly, watched children grow inside;
each disciple sleeping in the warm womb
of new belief, creating small worlds
in Your blood.  Only a woman, pregnant
with all humanity, could carry
that sin to the cross. As the soldiers pierced
Your side, You felt the veil split, tearing
the curtain between heaven and hell,
between free will and motherhood.  Dying,
Your tender womb fell apart in chunks,
creating universe after universe.

Deb Casey

## NOTE TO THE RESTLESS ROVER WITHIN

Hopeful to decode your subtle clues I rub
my belly to gather impressions     sift
what filters through the flesh
you stretch gauze sheer
—probing
to cup your skull deep
in my pelvis     to hold
intact    your thoughts and touch
your pulse     your head     settled firm
in the helmet of my bones               softening
to embrace your entry into this world—in one long
cerebral rush of imagination I anticipate you   arriving
                                    flushed into my open hands.
          *The baby want milk?* your sister inquires
of my bulging belly coaxing as she dips
my sun-warmed nipples
into her pink plastic tea-party cups
moistening the darkened areolas with sips
          to please you, Restless Sister. Charmed
          you rise to her voice. Whether drawn to drink
          from my moistened breasts or her rosy cups you flip:
my belly sways in east-west undulations—*awash!*
Breech Baby gone head high you take over
this house of the body
I once called my own. The house with an open door.

Cindy Frenkel

## SURRENDER AND ARRIVAL

Liquid gushing down my thighs
wakes me instantly, 5 a.m.,
trails my path, bed to bath;
my husband passes the phone.
I call Dr. Markowitz, my mother; sudden tears.

At the hospital,
Completely transverse,
Markowitz says, rubbing my shoulder,
Emergency cesarean, promises
I'll be fine, has me sign
that my death wouldn't be their fault.
My last moment on earth, in a room
with linoleum tile, fluorescent lights buzzing.
Wheeled to the O.R., teeth chattering,
Markowitz with me all the way, hand in mine;
strangers move mechanically
around my nakedness.

The anesthesiologist says
numb lungs will still breathe—
Let me know when you begin, I tell Markowitz.
I've already cut into you, he says,
then asks if I want to watch.
Watch? Yes I want to, Yes,
and the mirror rises like a revelation:
my blood splatters—he lifts the seven red layers
of my belly, slips his hands under my skin
as if reaching into the slit of an envelope.

Tiny birth-wax buttocks, shimmery,
and he turns the small body over,
A daughter!
I'm looking at myself
from above,
as they say one does in death,
morphine disguising pain,
joy and surrender so intense I can never
forget or remember fully.

Nadia Colburn

# THE PHYSICAL WORLD

For nine months
I anticipated,

as the other end
of pain,

a revelation:
a world turned

inside out.
Each inch I grew

marked a promise:
my present physical

certainty, my approaching
release.

And, indeed,
torn open,

I gave birth
to the end of ideas.

Beyond pain was born
no understanding,

beyond understanding
was revealed

no new knowing but
another body, robust,

which no thought
set screaming,

purple faced,
infuriated at air,

and no thought moved closer
to my breast,

and no thought closed
its thinly lidded

round brown eyes,
so soon worn out

by the unfamiliar light.

4

L.J. Sysko

## SITZ BATH

You won't
lower your body
into this inch and a half

of lukewarm water.
Tectonic plates
have shifted,

unbraided until
a small volcanic island
hisses—steaming,

breathing in the distance.
No, you won't
pink this puddle

with your stitched perineum.
No, you won't
soak in an All-Clad turkey roaster

like your friend
whose bathtub refused to fill,
settling into it like a handled carcass.

You will rock
in this chair
on ice packs

and a wadded pad
and burn:
surge and burn,

letting the lava run.
When you refuse the sitz bath's soothing,
when you ask him to fetch Preparation H,

tell him don't admonish me.
This is the new
topography, a small thorny vestige—

a jabbing rib
Adam won't ever
get back.

Meghan Smith

## THE FIRST FOUR WEEKS

I.
water showers down the night;
each trace of the event
the small metal grate
swallows salt and crimson
such a small mouth
to drink it all in, the hugeness
swirling around its edge
what used to nourish, sustain
emptied out,
this space we filled together.

II.
day drains
blue-veined balloon shining
stretched latex skin set to burst
roundness tied shut
with puckered rubber
hours sucked inward
light in the window narrows
shadow falls across a wrinkled heap,
shrunk down, dry
made to inflate again;
a shard of closet light watches
night fill.

III.
his arms fling wide
return to the tiny, heaving chest
a motion so much like a hug
a reflexive request
so connivingly designed
to make him more human,
keep me from drowning
him in the tub.

IV.
all of this
the work of culling
a smile from the rich earth
of sleep into waking
moments poised above him
watching splinters of brown
push through the molting blue
of his newborn eye

to know it only for me
to store it away
renew fallow exhaustion
where there is just enough
to find morning again.

Sarah Ghoshal

## IT ALL HAPPENED SO FAST

You some
how got from
lump to rolling
lump to crawling,
diving, standing
being with serious
intention, with
unabashed
optimism,
with total
belief in the
outcome.

I'm suddenly
alone
on the couch
as you figure
out the world
around you,
gather up the
soil from the
houseplants
in a cramped
fist and lift
it to your mouth
in slow motion,
daring me to
crumble it,
knock it
down like towers,
like unlit stars
falling heavy
from above.

Laura Sloan Patterson

## THE GIRAFFE

There is a cry across the hall. Not the toddler cry of *I want, I hate, You will do it now*, but an adult sob wrested into baby vowels. He squats on the floor, holding a rubber giraffe we once pretended French, a toy he hasn't touched since early teething. He's unearthed his own archeology, buried in a canvas bin, the culture of his babyhood, and there's an electrical crackle of shock. He folds her neck rhythmically and with each chiropractic bend, her keening squeak, and tears squeezed from his eyes. He cannot stop—the squeezing or the crying. He used to squeeze her like that and laugh deep in his body. When he tips his face up to mine, I see that it has happened: he knows I'm useless. He's two, the age of purest reason. But perhaps I am mistaken: was there another offense? Did they quarrel? Did she come home late, smelling of Snoopy and snow cones? I'll kill that giraffe bitch, I think. But later, while my son sleeps. I'll disembowel her and dance on her squeaker. Lying down at night, I see my boy's eyes in that moment of looking up, dimensional tunnels of sorrow. I mentally gather my tools: kitchen scissors, X-Acto knife, trash bags. But in the early morning I wake and know: I could hack legions of rubber giraffes, slit the evil girlfriend's tires, blackmail every admissions committee in the world. No use. It's not them but a sadness sipped from my own placenta, grown in the calcium of his bones. He grips the giraffe like the last bitter tuber in a burned-out forest, a rhizome he must carry on from here.

Kassie Rubico

## THE WAITING GAME

You decide to get the perishables last and make your way to the bread aisle, hoping there's nothing to set her off there, but balls always grab her attention. She reaches out to touch one of the colorful playthings. "Ball? I wanna ball." Big, brown eyes focus in on her new interest.

"Not now, Honey."

You select a few items. A loaf of bread, English muffins, then move on to the next aisle, leaving the balls behind. Perhaps she'll forget.

This aisle proposes Oreo Cookies, Cheezits, Fruit Roll-ups. Do you need ketchup? You can't remember, so you throw it in with the rest.

"Ball!"

She hasn't forgotten.

"Do you want a cracker?" you ask. Although you know distraction never works.

"No cracker. Ball!" The young voice is loud enough for a mother at the end of the aisle to hear, you recognize her from your older daughter's school. You look down, tighten your grip on the carriage, and push your way past her cropped bob.

In the front seat of the carriage, your daughter squirms, attempting to free herself of the black belt holding her hostage. A guttural sound warns you that it's about to begin.

You said no. You can't give in now, and it wouldn't matter if you did. Strong legs kick at whatever is in front of her – your stomach this time. Her back arches.
It starts.

Pickles, Ken's Steak House dressing, mayonnaise. Will you make it through this time? Four aisles to go. Sweat beads up on your brow despite the humming sound of the air conditioner.

You turn up the next aisle; pasta is on the left, ethnic food on the right. And the woman again. Loud shrieks replace the earlier whine. You check your watch because your oldest gets out of school in an hour, and one time you were late picking up, and she had to wait for you in the office. No tears, just kicking and screaming. The linguini will have to wait; you head for the exit sign.

Abandoning the half-full shopping cart next to the fresh flowers, you push though the automatic door. A clerk will probably have to put it all back, but you don't care.

The red minivan is parked close by. You've been here before and know what's necessary for a quick getaway. She tries to escape your arms, but the busy parking lot prompts a stronger grip. You don't bother strapping her into the car seat; she won't allow it. Her body flops on the floor. She has no idea what's happening. You do.

On the dashboard, red lights indicate that the radio is on, but there is no sound of music, only crying and the tune of her Stride Rites banging against the front seat. Her back bends, but she isn't a gymnast; she's a little girl who's lost control of her emotions You've read the book – several times. Temper tantrums take control over eighty percent of toddlers at one time or another. No yelling, no spanking, no guilt. It's a waiting game.

Finally, she begins to remember where she is and who she is there with. The crying stops. Intermittent sobs break the silence and shake the small body still lying on the floor. She is sorry. For what? It's not her fault, or yours.

You walk around the van and open the side door. Little arms reach out to greet you.

She nuzzles into your security. "I love you, Mommy."

Carrying her back into the store where the carriage is sometimes waiting, her chubby fingers feel comfortable around your neck as you fasten the strap around her belly. One final sob reminds us both that it's over.

You start again, with the perishables.

Wendy Mnookin

# CONSTELLATIONS

I lie in a hammock, sweating
glass of tea pressed to my forehead,
while somewhere down the street

a ball pounds on asphalt,
clatters against a backboard.
Shouts skid on humid air,

someone cheers, someone's
missed a shot. Do I miss
that noise and chaos, my kids

playing *Horse* in the driveway,
*Mother-May-I* on the lawn?
*If you lose by one, you still lose.*

The dog running circles, trying to herd,
barking her frantic commands.
*Please*, they'd beg

when I called them for dinner.
*Just a few more minutes.*
And really, what do I care?

Let them play until it's too dark
to see. Let them play
forever, refusing

to come in until the stars come out,
Lyre, Eagle and Swan, bright
burn in summer's nostalgia.

Sarah Evans

# WINDOW

Sunlight wanes, clouds filter out the last bits of pink and orange, the sky grays as I maneuver our family car out of the restaurant parking lot and toward home. I punch the down button for my automatic window and noises burst in: waves of wind rolling against my ears, the faraway rumble of car engines, the high-pitched heartbeat of crickets. Suddenly I'm 17 again, cruising my little town at night, always with the window down, my left elbow resting on the open frame, crawling down one street after another past gliding vehicles, prying street lights, sleepy houses, and persistent parking lots, not going anywhere in particular, satiated — compelled, even — by the immense possibilities of prowling about in the car while my parents snoozed in front of the TV at home.

These days, with my husband in the passenger seat and my two little ones tucked into their car seats in the back, I so rarely roll down my window that my toddler inquires, "Why did you do that, Mom?" I consider his question, but before I can respond, he asks, "Will you open my window?" I pause again, as I often do, wondering if there might be a negative consequence to fulfilling his request. Then the tendrils of wind, so familiar, tickle my face — and I lower his window, too.

Lisa Badner

# WATCHING ADOPTION VIDEO WITH MY 8 YEAR OLD

After a particularly shitty day in school
learning about immigration and then fighting with me
about reading logs, Minecraft and Hebrew School,
my son wants to watch his adoption video, again.
Given to us six and a half years earlier
by the Ethiopian social workers.
In the video, my son sees the hut he lived in, and his birth mother,
cows, a farm, an old grandmother.
The movie culminates in meeting his adoptive mother—me.
He is not even two but he's already my kid—
the Ethiopian courts had declared it.
All I'd seen before was a picture of his face.

Filmed by Elias, the cameraman at the Mussa center
in Addis Ababa, my son and I watch as the adoptive mother
doesn't know how to pronounce her son's name.
She is smiling like a nervous idiot.
She tries to hold the boy and he cries,
he has no interest in the bubble wand in her hand.
You see—he tells me
in our living room in Brooklyn,
now sitting on my lap,
you are a stranger,
some random person.

Laura A. Ciraolo

# THE USE OF ALL THINGS

In a conversation overheard
between a mother and a son, he says:
"Why do I need to know
about sines and cosines?
What will I ever use them for?"
The mother remains silent,
a sign her son would learn it,
whether he liked it or not.
His question was useless against her.
He would vent his frustration,
but he would do his homework.

When we limit ourselves
to what is utilitarian,
we should realize even
the clean lines and soft forms
of Shaker imaginations created
a beauty beyond plain and useful.
Where would we be
without sines and cosines?
Angles and triangles?
What is the sign of angels?
The impossible angles of a gothic cathedral?

As we lie in our recliners
numbed by the toxic news,
we are archeological wonders.
The dust of our flesh need only be brushed from our bones
to discover we are two hundred thousand years old,
just a walk out of the African savannah
to where even Neanderthal contemplated the infinite
burying their dead with flowers and adornments
carefully arranged.

Jenifer DeBellis

# THE DETROIT INSTITUTE OF ARTS

My daughter and I don't talk
anymore. She's too angry
and we can't seem
to find middle ground.

So we text each other.
Even today at the DIA
she texts me

it should be a crime to
drag someone to a place
like this against their will

> Her will, you mean.
> You might enjoy it.

not a chance -_-

So we walk in a silence
that blankets our life
like a volatile storm cloud
looking for a landscape
to unleash its full fury.

I stop in front of van Gogh's
*Bank of the Oise at Auvers*,
tugging her arm to tether her
to one spot for a change.

> See it? the way the
> trees sway?

She rolls her eyes, blows
her bangs from her forehead.

you forgot to cap your t

it must take a lot of talent
to paint thin men

> What about this one?

I stop in front of van Gogh's
*Self Portrait with Straw Hat*

van gagme

> Seriously, look at the
> detail, the dimension in
> the brushstrokes

It's clear the gallery attendant
following us is uncomfortable
with our closeness to the art.

                              I wish I could touch this
                              one—run my hand along
                              his jaw.

straw man in straw hat
yummmm

              We keep moving;
          it's what we both do well.
          I point out *Eleonora*
          *of Toledo and Her Son.*

lady in a rug with her
creepy chucky doll son

                              It's Bronzino's adaptation
                              of Madonna and Child.

let the nightmares begin

          Maybe this *is* a bad idea.

          We wander aimlessly now.
             I no longer point
          or pause to share. I turn
             to her; it's time
          to raise the white flag.

             But she's stopped
           in the gallery center,
              her chin thrust
          to the octagonal heaven
             of Tintoretto's
             *The Dreams of Men.*

             "Wow," she says,
              her arms limp
          at her sides, her jaw slack.

          "I know," I say back, no
             desire to look away
          from her enchanted face.

Andrea Potos

## DAUGHTER PEARL

Stashed behind teenage doors,
today's irritants
bristling through her,
might she be secreting
the nacre of who
she will be—
axis of each milky crystal
reflecting her,
refracting,
becoming silken light.

Maura Snell

## LEARNING

Hannah hooks a left onto route 30
and forgets to accelerate into the turn
then stutters into the flow of traffic
a little too much.
I remind myself to look at the sky.
My mother never took me out
when I was learning to drive.
It was dad who braved the passenger seat
of the '76 Chevy Malibu,
back when seatbelts
weren't always there, back when
cars were sofas wrapped in sheet metal
held together with duct tape from my mouth,
big enough for legs to sprawl in the backseat.
*Of course I took you driving* she says when I accuse her.
But I don't remember.
Why do our minds play games like that?
Why can't I recall her there in the passenger seat?
She must have gripped the door handle, must have
cursed under her breath as I shifted out
into the whirl. I mean, how did I become
my mother, invisible and perched,
looking up at the horizon?

Joanne Esser

# HIKE TO RATTLESNAKE LEDGE

Drive out of the city, your daughter behind
the wheel, bumper to bumper with all
the driven people chugging to their high-
rise cubicles. Veer away toward the blue
mountains you can barely see in the bright
haze of May. Roll down the window
just a crack. Weave up the winding road
past Douglas firs. Ascend to the unmarked
entrance between trees. Park the car,
gather water bottles, granola bars, sunglasses,
the jacket you will wear only for the first
ten minutes, then shed. Follow your daughter
to the trailhead where she has walked
many times before. This is her place. Let her
lead. Take it step by step, climbing steeply
as you talk. Don't be afraid to admit
your need to stop, drink some water.
Your legs will feel the work and respond.
Let your words rise up on cool drafts
of mountain air, crystalline. Heavy thoughts
released here will lift, be lighter to carry.
Face forward as you hike, brave enough
to approach questions you've never asked
aloud before. Pass slower hikers on the trail.
Let other hikers, young, eager, pass you.
Round the final curve, a switchback that
permits you to stand at last on the ledge.
What you've come all this way for.
Stand among the granite boulders high above
the valley, up at the tops of trees and look
out to the blue that goes on forever. Then
behold your daughter standing next to you:
the curious child she once was, the uncertain
adolescent, all the ages she has been, telescoped into
this strong woman who has brought you here.

Susan Vespoli

# SONOGRAM

When my daughter was a toddler
she stroked my cheek like it was the silk
edge of a blanket and pressed
the nipple-ends of soft balloons
into the plastic mouths of dolls

and when she grew breasts
boys flocked around her
like birds to our backyard
come to pluck seeds
from the center of a sunflower

and then her hands gained skill
to text friends, flick cigarettes
from the back porch, play Bad Fish
on guitar strings, and flip her middle
finger into the air like a slim bomb

until it finally folded back up, resting
in the cupped palm of the woman
who smiles at me from an exam table
with her eyes as bright as a camera flash
at the blip, blip, blip of a lit star that will be Molly.

# GENERATIONS

Unabashedly abundant, new growth clematis
spills across the river-side railing, sprouts
up through decking cracks, climbs and twists
tight tendrils about trellis and feeder, purple
flags aflutter effusively eclipsing

worn-to-shreds strips of sturdy old vine
holding steady yet weathered
from years of climbing, carrying on
the singular task of stringing sturdy structures
to root offshoots in the rich soil of home.

This intertwined tangle my dream of family
extended: roots sunk and shoots sprung
from the richness within, weathered fore-vines
supporting the new finding their own way
out, up and ahead.

Robyn Art

## WHAT I ASSUMED ABOUT THE AFTERLIFE

Were there any prior indications of danger?
Are you currently seeking recompense?
 Was the infrastructure always in question?
Were there any truths in the allegations?
 At what point does the fog become unknowable
 even to itself? What will you most remember?
What exactly might you mean by remember?
Do the days pretty much proceed
 at a pace that's  bearable  or, like
 forgiveness, glacial?
Do you have bad dreams?
Do you blame yourself?
Who are your people?  What is your favorite
 childhood trauma?  What were you doing anyway
in the wet arena, past the road,
through the torn and lucent fields?

HOW WE DARE NOT SEE                                    Margo Berdeshevsky

## DIVIDING LINE

<u>10:45</u>

Pink shorts, ironed carefully. Her shirt a field of linen blooming with violets. Moon-lit by five tiny silver buttons.  She adds a purple ribbon to her ponytail, clutched high in a rubber band. A few tendrils wisping by.

A day to fry eggs on the sidewalk, as New Yorkers say.

Fourth of July. Macy's closed. Gristedes closed. Down by the subway, the news stand's always open. Good day for a Pepsi. Guys ragging on each other. Working their smoke rings. Playing their lucky numbers.

Swings lifeless. Benches vacant. The big kids hanging at Orchard Beach.  Their little sisters off to Girl Scout camp. The Catskills for a week, sleeping in tents, whacking mosquitoes.

She's thinking of an ice cream. Later, maybe Loews for a movie. What's on today? Doesn't matter. Air-conditioned heaven.

NOON ----------------------------------------------------------------------------------

<u>1:00</u>

Shorts. The once-pink of them makes her nauseous. Ripped waistband. Hair glued to sweat-streaked neck. Ribbon long gone. Shirt a soggy dishrag headed for the trash. Four silver buttons.     One hole.

A day to fry eggs on the sidewalk.  A Fourth of July to remember. A taste like wet nickels. I hate you, she'd said.  She knew what that meant.

# FATHER'S DAY

Lessons on forgiveness came spilling into her navel
harsh messages invaded her body
the welcome laughter of a tickle turned to unwanted tears
taking away innocence
in silence she screamed     *wrong*

Forgive the gift of blindness
mother refused to see, refused to hear
childhood days lost in shadows
like Maya, her voice stilled
who would care, who wanted to listen to a dirty little girl

The father made-up the dead
with stiff white shirts and dark suits
Church Elder
Mentor to young men
Head of the house

His hands left dents inside her core
no longer a girl, not yet a women
somewhere in between

She learned to protect herself
calling his name to undo what he'd done
she breathed in Old Spice
his scent lingers in her hair, seeps into her skin

Yesterday she scarfed pills, spiced with Captain Morgan
the specter boogieman
stayed breaking her
into pieces
32 years later, pumped out, propped up
imperfect and broken
her truth uncovered

With Prozac and Celexa she writes letters to her father
begins to whisper to mother
can she hear her now?
her heart a frozen muscle manages mistakes and sex

On Father's Day
Hallmark does not have the words
shame, violation, a breach of trust
family secret still untold

What about sista?
Is there an incest gene?
What does love feel like?
What does love look like?
She tumbled into adulthood
mothering another generation
her child will not doubt her commitment
her child will not feel the fingers of invasion
her child will be free from victim branding

# SCRAPE

Scrape (scrāpe)  v. scraped   scrap·ing   scrapes
as in:  he scraped his elbow on the concrete sidewalk
where he fell  she ran  scraped his blood from the ground
a difficult task  like scraping together money to pay
an unexpected debt  she scraped pennies from the lining of his jacket
couch crevices  bottle caps  scraped donations from neighbors
scraping empties from the gutter  she scraped together his history
from relatives  grocery clerks  parish priest  as she waited for the dry cleaner
to scrape the food stains from his special occasion suit  the lipstick
from his staunch collar  scrape away his foolishness:  not being satisfied
he scraped his-self into another man's scraped together household
where the bullet waited   now she waits by her door for the seamstress to come
scrape together the sullied edges of the hole in his one good shirt  she scraped
together her children to follow the hearse to the crematorium to collect his urn
the one she opens on her worst days to scrape the bloodied dirt into his ashes
chanting all the spells she ever knew to make him breathe again
so she can stop teaching her daughters how to scrape together one good man
from the scraps who have lined-up to prey on her altar

Elisabeth Weiss

## CITY OF PROMISE

*Metal. Granite. Uproar. Racket. Clatter. Automobile. Bus. Subway. El. Burlesque.*
*Grotesque. Café. Movie-theater. Electric light in screeching maze. A spell.*
—A. Leyeles' Yiddish poem of 1918, "New York," (translated by Benjamin Harshav)

Nothing, not even the past, remains constant for long.
One kind of Jew gave rise to another,
as did the various languages in the burial grounds:
first Portuguese then German,
Yiddish, Ladino and then English.
And then you, Hungarian, Russian, Polish,
tenement Jew. First to Williamsburg, then
Bushwick then Greenpoint
Riding your bike the wrong way on a one way street,
Renting a studio and filling it with the tools of your labor,
Drinking in a park on the East River
Spending the night in lock up.
Speeding through lights, fire in your belly,
Learning every street your grandfather and great ever walked
With enthusiasm for jewels in the garbage
And the fun and the razzmatazz of the old clubs.
You stitch delicate embroidery on the buttons of Uncle Louie's
Ace High Belt and Buckle Company,
Pushing racks in the garment district
Delivering down the sidewalks:
awls, leather sewing machines, lasts.
Your wheels turn in urgency to the noise and speed of
an overarching interpretation of what it means
to do the city justice, to bridge a leitmotif.
rivets of imagination rule,
compounding metals and matter
approaching the glorious material at hand.
Entangled in one of the greatest relationships
you'll ever have with an oversized personality
between the New World and the vast number
of inhabitants, America's first great ghetto.
And to you, enterprising, starry-eyed,
it is a homecoming of sorts.
Weave now and come to understand later
how the guiding hand fabricates our fortunes.

Ann Fisher-Wirth

# IN THAT KITCHEN (SHE SPEAKS TO HERSELF)

*Oh Christ, that night should come so soon.*
—William Carlos Williams

You grew up in a kitchen where salt and pepper arrived in corncob shakers and oil and vinegar dressing lived in a cruet with a little skirt. Gingham curtains, starched and bleached and pressed free from all grease and smoke, fluttered in good morning America. But that was a kitchen that never interested you, a kitchen of mom and Chuck and little Davie, of Rex the cocker spaniel and Bluet the parakeet. It's gone now, gone, gone, gone. Smoke stains the blue corridors. Chuck joined the Army and was killed in Vietnam. Little Davie bought a motorcycle. Thank God he learned to think for himself, now he's a doctor in Tangiers.

Think of the lies you all were told about sex and history and America. Think of the body. It wants to lie all open, salt-stained, rain-scarred, the body wants its forgetfulness and honey. You rock back and forth, shoulders hunched, smoke rising from the one cigarette you allow yourself, stained, scarred, once-visionary woman, good morning America gone now, guns massed at the borders once again, churches burning, dogs howling, you in the private theater of your own film noir.

In that kitchen, despite the official sunshine, soup boiled up with the bones of winter birds, cook-sweat slid down the windows, and the mothers cooked the death of things. That is a role you do not need, not in this world of ruined cities. Put your jacket on, walk out, take to the beds of lovers. The Never Rains Always Pours corncob shakers are clogged with bones and feathers and ash. Take to the streets of this our damned and doomed America.

# I SEE YOU

Sitting on a park bench,
With one eye on the playground,
I see you
Wiry, thin, happy
Racing down the field
Click
And you are
A dead 12 year old
Black male, shot dead
Splashed across the
Front Page
Dead on the ground.
Ripped away
My empty arms cry out
To you in pain

Standing in front of the house
Talking to a neighbor
I see you
Wiry, thin, laughing
Running across the crosswalk
To meet a friend
The sound of
Screeching brakes
And you lay there
A dead 12 year old
Black girl, dead in the street.
Your story never makes the paper.
You are just
No longer there.
An empty space in my soul

It was over a candy bar
Killed by a cop
Drunk with power.
It was over a white driver
Drunk
In a black neighborhood

I still see you.

# BLACK LIVES MATTER: A MAMA'S PERSPECTIVE

What words/what language do we use to discuss with our children the non-indictment of the officers who killed 12-year old Tamir Rice? How do I discuss with my 11-year old son yet another incident of injustice against a black child? How many times in my two sons' lifetime will we have this all too familiar conversation in our household? How do I explain to my sons that "a perfect storm of human error" is a double standard? How to explain the likelihood that white men who commit violent crimes and use guns will get to leave those crime scenes alive and unharmed, while innocent black children and adults, who are perceived as "threatening" and have a toy gun or candy in their hands or are empty-handed, will most likely get killed by police or wannabe police, while no one is held accountable again and again? How do I make absolutely clear to my sons that their lives have so much value, when our judicial system keeps saying otherwise? How do I not break down in tears or scream or smash something against a wall, when all I want to do is protect my sons/our collective sons and daughters from racist folks who see them as a threat? When will a black child be allowed to be just that, a child at play or a child walking home and not somebody's target? What adequate healing words can I offer to my 11-year old son when he tells me he is not shocked, but that he is very upset, that once again there is no indictment after the murder of an innocent black child? Why is this now a familiar part of his vocabulary? How do we heal and uplift our children when there is so much hurt and distrust? Every time my 11-year old son asks me *Mommy why does this keep happening to black folks and why is no one being held responsible?* why do my answers feel insufficient? How do we wrap our children in love and then let them walk out the door, when we know there are people in the world who actually think it is "reasonable" to find the presence of a 12-year old black child threatening? How is this acceptable? How is it that I can see all the hope and promise and beauty of the future in every black child that crosses my path, while others look at our children and feel threatened? Why does parenting black children in 2015, and trying to keep them safe and alive, feel just as risky and dangerous as it must have felt to parents all those decades ago? Why is loving a black body, a black girl, a black boy, a black woman, a black man, a political act? Why y'all why?

Emily R. Blumenfeld

## A SUMMER TRUTH TELLING

one truth
        anti-racism speaks truth to the brutality
        of institutionalized white supremacy
another truth
        whenever anti-racism vanishes from commitments to
        human needs and equality we are collectively diminished
heart truths
        dividing lines between we and not us grow by their own division
        a mathematics of endless division leaves less than our humanity
trauma truth
        the dehumanization of racism is more than dangerous
        before, during, beyond this summer
truth telling witness
        each mother's terror for her child's safety
        each mother's grief for her child's life
        held within all our hearts

## PERSEID, OR THE FIRST DAY OF SCHOOL

During the meteor shower the sky flows with honey.
Inside, I drink hot tea from my sunflower mug. I read about
the trapped miners. The fungus growing on their pale skin.
The pick-up truck 2,000 feet underground, with a good front

seat to die in.  In the morning my 5-year-old will walk
to kindergarten, a bouncing pink backpack with arms and legs.
The men divided a slice of peach 33 ways. They learned how
to pray. They had a Cap of Darkness to make themselves

invisible. They put Medusa's head in a magic bag made of diorite
and chimneys that did not have ladders. The paths of their boots
in the mud, like the pretty streaks of comet dust, do not last long
before blackness resumes with its oversize pencils and small

chairs. The destroyer. The beheader. The miners rose like astro-
nauts to their constellations of lovers' arms. I do not go outside.
The stars fall and turn me into stars and somehow we will walk home
together in the hot noon sun with bologna and almost no shadows.

Charlotte Mandel

# TYPHOON HAIYAN

*The Philippines, November 2013*

Blinded by salt torrents
swallowed into white
heart of whirlwind

houses shattered to peels of bark
palm trees stripped
of fronds coconuts all

fruits of labor  mangoes rice tamarind
chickens pigs wild
eagles tarsiers hornbills

electric wires wooden
shellacked bowls trays
wares tourists pack into airplanes

fathers  mothers  infants
borne into primeval
birth waters

roaring them back.

# GLOBAL CLIMATE CHANGE

It was the summer we went to Giverny, saw
the lily pads, the gardens that bloomed
in the paintings; like walking into a familiar
dream, we knew what came next
before we went around the bend.
What we didn't know, what we
couldn't know, were the dark
clouds gathering, storms in the east,
buildings in flames.  Melting
ice caps, weather running wild.
Cracking glaciers falling into the sea,
permafrost that isn't, hillsides
crumbling, ice that held the rocks
in place giving way.  Canals
in the Netherlands that fail to freeze,
no regattas, ice boating, races
for the silver skates.  In Canterbury,
prayers rise like small birds, bells
announcing God's voice in the fallen
world.  But towers can fall, empires
replace each other, and peace is as fleeting
as pink and white clouds floating on a lily pond,
halfway between earth and sky.

## HOLIDAY INN

There's a Holiday Inn on Delancey Street.
Can't find parking on Avenue D.

This is not a rant.
It's not *boo hoo the city has changed bye bye Bleecker Bob,*
*Pizza Box J & R  go away blue buildings come back garbage strike.*

No need for all that.
There's a Holiday Inn on Delancey Street.
Can't find parking on Avenue D.

I don't remember what was once on that corner.
Maybe it was the children's store with the clothing
so cheaply made that a red polka dot dress I'd bought
for my daughter burst into flames in the drier and burnt
all of her pink and white blankets and socks.

Who goes to a Holiday Inn on Delancey Street,
at the foot of the Williamsburg Bridge, where
methadone clinic patients drink extra sweet
coffee with donuts and carry the Daily News?

Once the only cars on D were up on blocks.
We walked through there coming from the day
care center the same year the clothes burned.
My daughter learned how to climb steps on the
bandshell, and said the word *water* at the pool.
We'd ride the F Train to Coney, she'd scream
SEE WATER as we pulled into Stillwell Avenue.
Other than that, it was a very bad year, but
at least there were no Holiday Inns on Delancey
and if I'd had a car I could have parked it
on Avenue D, kept the tires if I gave a drug
dealer a ride or two, maybe driven out to Coney
yelling SEE WATER as we crossed the bridge,
maybe would have made it a better year.

This year isn't bad at all.
I drive my car to Coney Island.
My clothes are not on fire.
I don't worry about much any more.

There's a Holiday Inn on Delancey Street,
Can't find parking on Avenue D.

I circle slowly around the neighborhood.
Eventually, I go home.

## cards & curiosities

at 5
the chocolate bar
will close, gone, done,
run down to
as the pink neon sign says,
'get some,' the line
too long, go next door
to cards & curiosities,
in a month, also done, and
elie, back of the register,
smack dab center in welter mix of
retablos, mounds and piles of
sharks teeth trilobites skulls head
day of dead singerdancerboxers hanging
twisted wood & glitter ornaments, dinosaur bones,
insects in amber 45 million years old,
semi-precious stones, pop-up jack-in-boxes,
elie tells me how one grandfather
makes it thru the camps in poland, then,
walking up to his own front door,
'the locals,' as elie puts it,
shoot, the entire family
wiped
       3 1/2 years in romanian slave labor,
the other grandfather,
now its 1944, the nazis routed
but theres a kinda no-mans land
for a few hours, this grandfather
and a friend can take the train
to town, but its saturday, a dispute:
elies grandfather says
its saturday. we have to observe
the sabbath.
the friend goes, the nazis
return, everyone in town slaughtered,
elies grandfather w/2 pals
take the train
next morning, bury
the bodies best they can, and survive

7pm yesterday james locks cards & curiosities,
june 1st today by 2 pm: white on black sign, huge:
sinvin/bold solutions.brilliant results. RETAIL FOR
LEASE.

4/26-6/1/15
eve packer

Margo Berdeshevsky

## DAILY BREAD

My mama fell from her chair
dead when the blood knot called her in.

A poet tried to recite Our Father when she
fell, couldn't find the words in English

now but her childhood French
hid there—somewhere—she grabbed

until the mind caught the blackbird's
wing and she prayed again—*daily bread*

My new neighbor comes to morning's latch
lonely—*my ex wife is in hospital,*

*blood to the brain, she's lost all speech—*
*we have a child* —and—
*je voudrais coucher avec vous* —

All his darting-rose-tongue truth soars
before I pour the second brew

whisper *no,*
where the purple irises lean in
where blackbirds come hungry

In a precipice town where
once, a hermit hid— pilgrims

come step after step up its cliff
of stairs on their knees —

penitents' chained
locks,      broken

a candle-blacked virgin's bell
—there— rung with no rope
for miracles

—I climb
for a God who hides

—to stop,

all the way down.

Margaret Rozga

# THREE WOMEN SHARE TWO SANDWICHES

Kathryn pointed out the red at the upper right, then moved her hand down the page and to the left, counting, one, two, three. Three uses of red. That satisfied her.
I asked about the direction of the crows' flight, sometimes up, sometimes down, sometimes….
    "Sometimes away," she said.
    I liked the way she gave me words I needed. I noticed other details: the crows' wings, the fluff of their feathers, the line of the road, the corn chips they swooped down to gather.
    "I like three," Kathryn announced. "Or five."
    My poet friend Carolyn clings to advice some workshop leader once proclaimed: avoid three. I didn't repeat this to Kathryn. It didn't seem true now. Nor was it kind to contradict her, and kindness flowed as easy as our conversation, even though we had been strangers before Mary brought us together.
    We three had lunch, sharing the two huge turkey sandwiches Mary bought before we went up into the mountains to Kathryn's. Kathryn couldn't meet us in town. She had worked all morning illustrating a book she and her granddaughter Darby designed and wrote. At noon she was ready for a rest, though not up to fixing lunch.
    We talked about our mothers. Mine hugged me the morning I returned from Alabama. A friend had picked me up at the airport. It was late. I unlocked the door and, exhausted, slept on the couch in the living room. In the morning, I woke to my mother sobbing, hugging me and sobbing. That was the first I knew she had worried about me, her headstrong daughter, working on a voter registration drive in 1965 rural Bullock County, near George Wallace's home town.
    Mary's mother had a fit the first time Mary was arrested, but then one Mother's Day, Mary stopped at home after having been at a rally in Madison earlier in the day. She and her mother watched TV, the news, Mary being interviewed. They switched the channel, Mary being interviewed, and again on the third channel, Mary. Oh, wow, her mother said. Proud. Of Mary. That was in May. That August her mother died. Mary was in Nevada, demonstrating at the site of nuclear testing.
    Kathryn's mother married a year after high school graduation. A man twelve years her senior had romanced her, took her to plays, concerts, dinner, celebrated her, cut her meat. She was swept off her feet, married him. He did not believe in any form of birth control. Within six years, they had five daughters, and then he died. The daughters, Kathryn one of them, were all still young. Kathryn's mother never showed much interest in her daughters' many accomplishments, though they kept hoping.
    When the girls were grown and on their own, their mother became president of the library board. She did such a marvelous job that when she died, the library board named the new president "acting president." Kathryn's mother, though dead, retained the title of president.
    Kathryn, a speech therapist, went to British Columbia to work, to live, rugged and free. Met Rand, a lawyer. Moved to Alaska. Worked as his assistant, cases to protect people's water rights. Then, so much assisting, what else, she became an artist.
    Two friends, two friends, two strangers. Three in all. Talking what changed their mothers' lives, what changed their own: peace, civil rights, marriage, marriages, the Alaska bush, art. Turkey sandwiches. Tea in cups from other mothers grateful to Kathryn for helping their children speak, helping them read.
    A catch in my throat. Kathryn's eyes tearing again. Mary laughing.

# CHANGE
*8-12-2015*

This summer when I finally thought I had the time off to write my memoir, clear up and rearrange my little apartment on the sixth floor, paint, swim and dream with the vacation days from my job at the non-profit youth and community center where I had put in 24/7 for the past fifteen years, the center lost its funding.

My salary was cut in half, I lost over sixty paid vacation days, but I still had the medical health insurance; and for a Stage IV breast cancer survivor still with three tumors in the remaining half of a right lung and now two new tumors on the thyroid, twelve doctors I either see every year, six months or every three months, plus the fistful of medications I must take daily, that was not a bad thing to have the health insurance.

To ensure I kept that part time job, that health insurance, I now needed to raise funds as quickly as possible for a new arts program.

Part of me is grateful at sixty-three years of age to have this part time job and health insurance; yet part of me wants to, to quote Bruce Springsteen's song, "I want to spit in the face of these badlands…"

I'm not wealthy. Having worked most of my life in community based, non-profit organizations, that's what happened: I have no profit! I began to worry about bills to pay, co-pays for medication, blood tests, scans, rent, food. At three hundred dollars a week can I make ends meet?

On weekends I'm taking care of my daughter's ninety-six year old grandfather, who she nicknamed "Dada" when she began speaking as a toddler. Grocery shopping, preparing three meals a day, housework, laundry, exercises, walks, talks, appointments; and I say God bless all caretakers!

My Tribal kids (young people I mentor) or their friends or friends of their friends call from the youth center:

-We visit the immigration lawyer to apply for Temporary Protective Status because I have promised his visiting parents I would help their son.

-Another student needs to be readmitted back into City University because he has been dismissed due to poor grades in his freshman year from working full time to pay for a room when his father kicked him out of the house in the midst of his chemo treatment.

-I wait to hear the results of a pathology report from another young person who has received surgery for the removal of a cancerous mass.

-Refusing therapeutic help, another one of my Tribal kids tries a vitamin regimen and smokes. I offer to accompany him to the psychiatrist but am told, "I'll think about it."

-A promising young painter returning to NYC after graduating abroad needs studio space to continue the development of her art work. I make calls to friends inquiring what and where to find available studio space for gifted emerging young artists.

-I write numerous Letters of Reference and edit final papers, thesis, personal statements, resumes and serve as a reference for jobs, internships, colleges my Tribal kids are seeking.

-Here, I have to say that one of my Tribal kids worked hard and repaid a loan that will cover my three month's rent once he heard my salary was cut in half!

-A young woman who calls me her "Chinese mother" and many more of the Tribe offer and want to know how they can help. Thanking them, I tell them I have to figure that out, but no worries, I will call upon them, my dear Tribal kids!

Several weeks ago at four in the morning my young daughter calls from her local police station and says, "Mama! The house (where she was renting an apartment with a friend) burnt down to the ground and the car exploded! I lost everything but I'm okay. I have my life!" I thank the universe for sparing my lovely daughter. I piece together and wire her funds.

Running, I'm exhausted. I am running full court back and forth, back and forth; I can't lose the ball. Day and night I'm riding the bloodlines of this city's subway system; sometimes three boroughs in a row.

The neighbors call. "Part of your mother's house is leaking from the roof. You need to check this out." I hear disapproval in their voices and tell them I will take care of this. Note: call our friend the contractor.

The organization I volunteer for that fights police brutality calls to see if I can make a six foot banner for the rally next day at Union Square on the one year anniversary of Michael Brown's killing in Ferguson. After Dada's dinner, I head downtown and work on the banner till four in the morning, go home and fall flat on my face in bed. I will always support those seeking justice for family members and friends killed by this country's occupying civilian army, the police.

My two sisters call from out of town and tell me to stop and rest. I tell them it's not so simple.

I always think it takes the same energy to say "Yes" as to say "No," so why not say "Yes".

I also believe "Love saves the day" and I tell my Tribal kids, "The heart is a muscle. So use it and you'll see how strong the love flows from and to you."

Hah! My own laundry lies in bags next to bags of clothing and books I want to donate to the women's shelter and local public library, piles of papers and manuscripts to be sorted and filed, my refrigerator is empty. The memoir goes unwritten for days at a time. I worry about paperwork, bills, make lists of things I must do---yesterday. I vow to myself: I will write a kick-ass book and I will play Lotto! And swim! And paint!

While washing dishes, the lists of what to do in my head grows bigger and longer. I'm spinning.

Dada comes into the kitchen. He says, "Stop. Stop what you're doing and come here."

I follow him to the open window. The sun is setting over the river. Red orange and pinks in a brilliant turquoise blue sky with one lone puffy cloud drifting slowly across the sky. The air is crisp.
A ship sits still in the middle of the river anchored. A barge moves slowly down river. Birds swoop into the distance.

We watch silently as the red orange light sinks into the horizon, a line above the shimmery steel blue water. The moon rises.

"Another day," Dada says.

Yes, a new tomorrow.

Robyn Art

## FURTHER QUESTIONS FOR THE AFTERLIFE

What do you mean by "murmurous?"
Is it, "without plans to attack?"
Had you already left the arena?
What was the native dress in question?
What of that particular hovering?
Why not return to the crash site?
Why not root there in the hyacinth
for the tiny broken clasp?

# AGAINST MELANCHOLY (AS HILDEGARD DEFINES IT)

When black bile settles in me like an army
of buzzing flies, muscles stiffen from my right
shoulder to ear. My eye squints, brow furrows.
Before I realize it, I've inched forward, shifted
in my seat, tilted my hips. The ache lists.
Worse? Exhaustion, as if steel molecules,
subtle in my blood, weigh me down. Lethargic
twilight—my body's ambiguous indigo.

The cause, Hildegard said, is knowing good
but choosing otherwise. Was it my satisfaction
at a loathed-one's bad news? The catch
of judgment at a colleague's words? The friend's
request for help I dismissed as drama?

Hildegard, I want to throw off sorrow
and move bitterness straight on through
this flesh. Return me, balanced, to the Table.
I'll bandage a nosegay of primrose over
my chest, its heart-shaped petals morphing
into dream butterflies. I'll sleep with stones
of onyx and agate against my skin and wake
with cool bruises. I'll sprinkle nutmeg into soup,
oatmeal, coffee. I'll drink quenched wine.
I'll gift my jewels to friends, share flowers
with strangers, invite an enemy to tea.
O Inspired One! I'm ready to swim, open-
lipped and kicking, to the surface of my life.

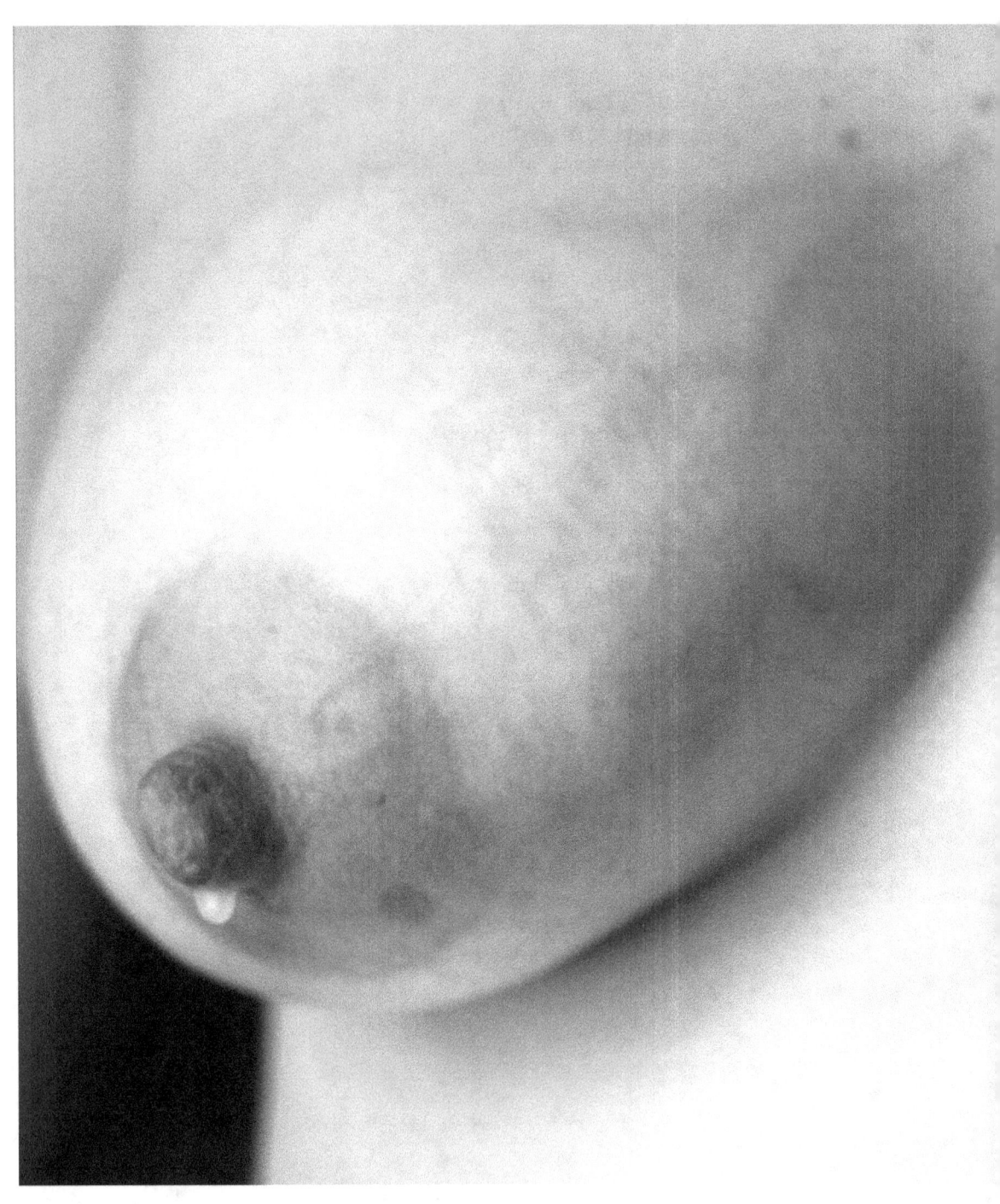

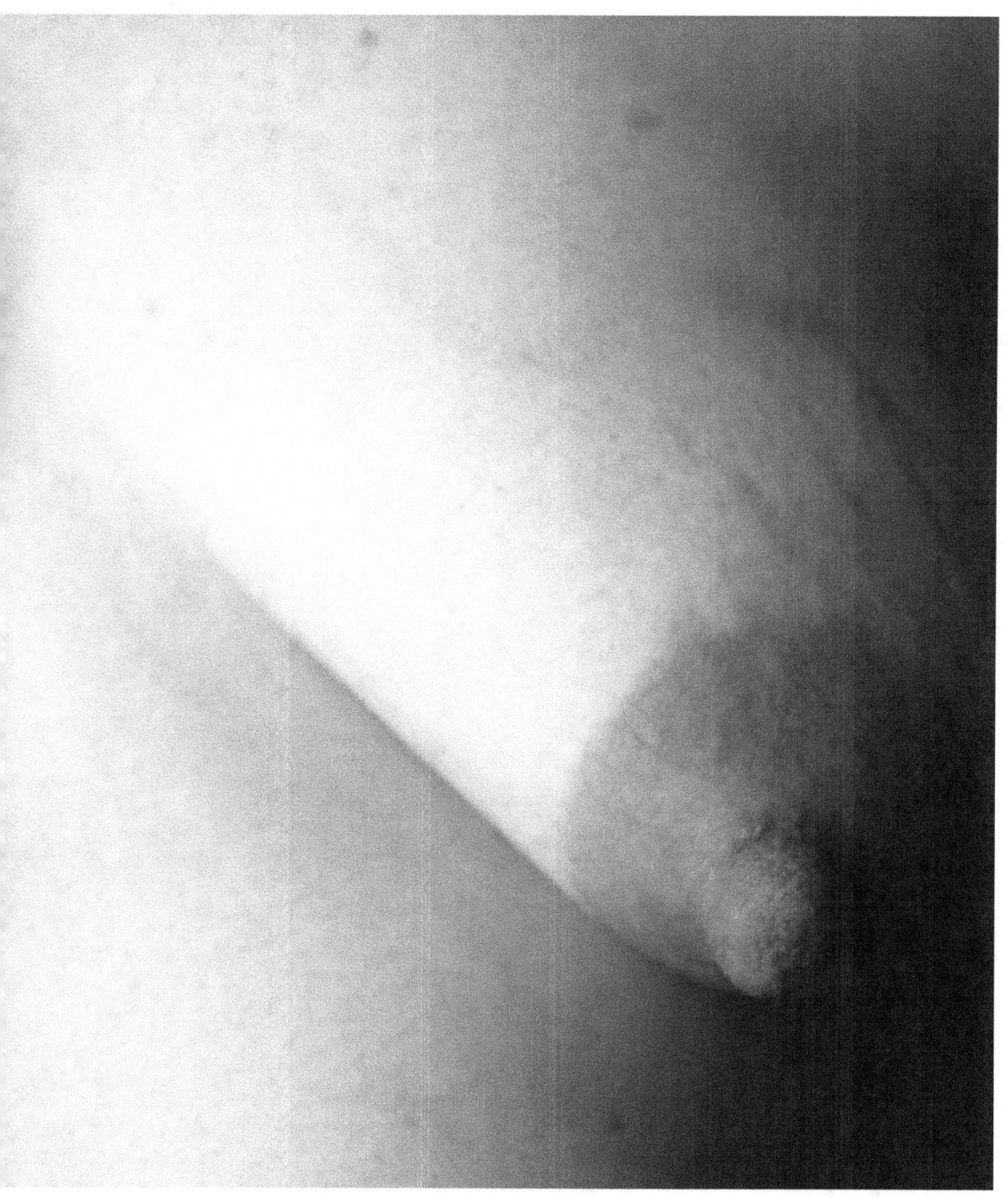

ABOUT TO BURST/COMPLETELY DRAINED                    Megan Wynne

Gwen North Reiss

## SEPTEMBER AFTERNOON

And gold spills out of the sky
fishnetting the trees and the air
the season beginning its departure.
Impossible not to notice—
the mind wants to hold
onto it like someone
you won't let step on a plane.
And a hunger
you can't do anything about
opens like a flower.

Hilde Weisert

# ARS POETICA

"I learned to talk from my mother," I said,
and was startled: Doesn't everyone?
But "learned from"—
as if it were playing the piano,
or making the sylsalat at Christmas?
But it was: Her speech,
invented for me, her patience
letting my mouth and tongue
work the vowels, open
and open, then clench consonants
hard in my teeth, all nibbled edge,
and me still making of it a gibberish,
a babble; a glottal soup,
a drool;

My answering nothing but a rhythmic rumination
of nonsense syllables. But she kept on,
now a whisper, now a song, and in a while
the words became words: *Epitome*
and *punctilio, modicum*
and *masterly*; plenty of slang
like *vamoose* and *delish*, and play
in the *"Ditto"* that either one
could say, and smile (a secret).

This language of the days
of our small world, dangled from,
rolled in, colored and toddled,
and finally slept on, a pillow,
the sun,

is now so many vocabularies ago, fields
of cultivated speech—

But with this odd sentence I remember
what came first,
the ravishing world she made
me take, word by hungry word,
and how much more there is to tell
in our original language.

Tess Barry

## BIRTH RE-ORDER

The baby for six years
the seventh daughter, the ninth
child of ten, the family pet
doted upon, adored,
almost ruined, until finally
one August day Dad called
at sunrise. I listened
from my bed, got the name,
put on my red tennis shoes,
walked door-to-door
the entire neighborhood,
calling, *We have a boy, James.*

The Kindermans, half-dressed
and half-asleep, coaxed me
into their living room, called home,
gave me a drink and broke
the news: *you're not the baby anymore.*

Carol Dorf

## ADA

With a mother tongue, there are always exceptions to the rules. Not so with the language of mathematics, *une langue bien faite.* While in a given context mathematical notation is consistent, as the context changes a symbol such as, -1, for example, can take on additional meanings. Ada Lovelace's mother encouraged mathematics as a boundary against what was suspected to be an inherited poetic disposition, the type that sent her father, Lord Byron, off to Greek Islands with floating landscapes of ocean and lovers. Ada Lovelace's fantastical imagination followed a mathematical bent – flying machines and then calculating engines. Her mother's attention not a waste.

Remember Ada with a language.

Ana C.H. Silva

## HALTER TOP

my cousin put it on me         anyway
      against       my shyness

she found it in a drawer
    a red scrap
        strappy

how it let air pass over my arms
          and back
    only a thin tie behind
 me

   my mother would never dress me in tops like that --

    shirts that let the sun and wind touch
      your skin where you can't

see it coming—

## STARLIGHT

When Big George offers me
a mint, it's not enough for me
to take the mint. She wants to
see me pull the mint out of
its noisy plastic wrapper and
put the mint into my mouth,
until it dissolves. Completely.

I wanted
to want
the starlight
mint from
the dark of
her purse
where lipstick
lived, with
tissue packs and
lotion tubes
and clear
plastic rain
bonnets.

I used to want the mint,
but when I got older the mint
made my teeth feel fuzzy so
when she'd try to give me the
mint, I'd shake my head and
take one of those—
dirty looks instead.

I wanted
to want
the starlight
mint from
the dark of
her purse where sweetness—
and obligation lived.
I wanted to want
what she wanted
me to want, but
I couldn't
I didn't want it.

Cindy Veach

## ON THE GRAIN

Because I ignored the bias,
        cut the fabric off-grain,

clothes I sewed never fit,
        bunched at the knees, pulled

at the hips, pinched at the waist.
        Because I wasn't like my mother,

who could hold straight pins
        in her mouth and talk,

no matter how hard I tried
        to follow patterns

there were always flaws,
        things I should have ripped

out, done over. When she tried
        to show me, step by step,

I was impatient, took short cuts,
        every project failed

to live up to the Simplicity
        pattern book promises—

skinny-limbed girls in ruffled bikinis,
        peddle pushers, mother-daughter outfits.

I couldn't make us match. She'd look up
        from her converted treadle,

over the gold letters that spelled SINGER,
        wind a bobbin, thread the machine,

take her seam ripper
        to my botched hip hugger miniskirt.

She found and flushed
        my drugs. Intercepted and tore up

letters on blue paper from a boy
        I thought I loved.

Why did I think
        I could guess at yardage,

fudge seam widths?
        Why did I refuse the seam ripper

only to tear apart what I'd made
        with my hands?

And now she hands me
        this sturdy fabric Mémé wove

in the mills of Lowell.
        I fold it on the grain,

warp to warp, weft to weft, place it
        in my basket of remnants.

## GROWING UP

My shoes abandoned on the front stoop
told my mother everything she needed to know.
As she clapped them together, releasing the peaches
caked on the bottoms, and shook her head,
a smile crossed her face. 1305 Brazos St.
Texarkana, Texas stained her speech,
"That boy was in the orchard again."

I'd walk through like a blind man feeling
for large round semisoft drupes and listen
to the squash of fermented ones under my feet.
Freeing myself from the isolation
of never being alone, my mother would hear
the back door click from her bed.
 "There he goes again," she'd tell my father.

I always picked the fruit straight off the tree.
To be the one that stressed the branch,
broke off the fruit, bit into the soft skin,
and tasted its sweet insides was the pleasure
of having something grow just for you.
Sometimes I'd meet up with my girl,
moonlight was always better than the movies.

The orchard's foliage covered my presence
from passing cars and nearby neighbors.
I'd get some local boys together and have bon fires
right there in the orchard, burning branches
that weren't ours and boundaries
only my mother suspected I was crossing.

Ann E. Michael

## BICENTENNIAL SUMMER

The summer I worked
on the New Jersey Turnpike
I wore a vertical-striped shirt
my name embroidered bright
red on the pocket like
a modern-day Hester Prynne
the only girl gas jockey
on the plaza, thin &
tanned like a workman
wearing neoprene-soled
boots, and radio disco blared
all day in the little
glass booth where we shared
the credit card imprinter
while customers simmered
in long slow lines,
radiators steamed
the air liquid with heat &
diesel fumes scribbling,
blurred by sunlight,
everyone irate
over the price of fuel,
fighting with their kids.
Early morning wasn't bad
but after the sweat-haul
of days breathing Exxon,
the sun starting a brawl
in my brain, or a week of rain,
I moved my allegiance from
the cynical romanticism
of lyrical songwriters & learned
what rock & roll could do
for me, I earned
the need to unpeel myself
from myself at day's end
after being plugged in
to a blue-collar slog,
bored and most of all lonesome
& the blues and Motown
drove me there song by song
with the stark sweet appeal of

the baritone sax's gut-clutching moan
of restive love
and the bass-beating-pavement
shuddering up my legs meant
I felt ways I didn't dare move
on those small islands of cement
with the pumps fuming,
counting gallons behind my back.

Alison Condie Jaenicke

## RED STRING OF FATE

Above her belly and below her heart
she tucked her yearning for you, irrational
hope that you'd come back. She flew to the windy shore
on which you'd trained, Rhode Island's rocky coast,
claimed a front row seat in the gym to watch.
The wood floor boomed as newly minted
officers marched under flags and flat-top hats
Each one's hair equally gone
Each one's face equally steeled
processing toward her in line after line of men
stripped to the essence, rebuilt in white dress uniforms.
She tried to snap your picture like you'd asked
She took one, then you came toward her and she saw
It wasn't you
Just someone very like you
And each time she tried, it wasn't you
until her hand on the shutter began to shake.
She cried because you were gone
and afterward when she told you,
you complained she had ruined your day.
*Someone has to do this*, you said.

Later when she left you, your response:
*I suppose you're saying, shit or get off the pot—*
*so we should marry?*
She knew: *Someone will make a soldier's wife*
*but not me.* Her "no" felt small
but it was all she had. She flung it seaward,
this crimson thread that floated
toward foam where a gull
swooped to pluck it.
She has made a habit of throwing
refusals into the air, imagines
a nest somewhere
lined with red.

## SHAPE

In the twenty-ninth year of my life, it is a beautiful
fall. The leaves have grown brighter and brighter
and now cover the ground with their fire and also hold on
to a few trees and glow, all the time. As if it were always to be
sunset and all the air radiance.

Things are as they should be.
As I have wished they would be as I walk along, myself, in my life
down the street where we have come to live,
my husband, I and our child. And where, for a while,
I have not thought to ask whether I am happy,
which means I have not wanted for happiness.

Beside the yellow house we see a black cat asleep
in a ball, and already I am thinking,
What is it that makes things, lives, fall suddenly
into shape, when we pass the man I met last week,
whose name I didn't hear, with his normal-looking
wife and his girl, saying, "Look at me, look how well I rake,"
we all being ourselves beneath the chinese maple,
and someone planting bulbs for next year's spring.

**

Last night at dinner, our friend told us he has given up
on love. Or not on love, but on the perfect love
that will be all that he desires.
He is having the name of his ex-wife
removed from his back.
A year ago, living in a small town, in coastal Maine,
he was desperate. Each morning he woke alone.
Far off, when he woke early, in the stillness,
in the autumn, or when it had snowed, he heard the surf.
As if it were he going in, going out.
And the house so empty.
As if one could be no live thing. With no heartbeat.
With nothing one's own.

**

Walking down the street, this is all there is of brightness
I will know. Looking at my life, I see it so clearly.
My husband. My son. And suddenly it seems I am the shape
of the wife on the street wanting willingly
to change nothing. Wanting willingly to own
nothing. Wanting somehow to resist form.

I once thought my life was a preparation.
Now I think of the amputees, how they go on
when the strong ones get killed off, their body
not its natural shape, their life undrawn.
In the book I have bought, a man,
already blind in one eye, steps on a land mine which blows
off his leg and he does not complain.
But I am not sure I can believe this,
that what is his is his so fully.

**

All around me everything has so far to fall.
When it gets dark the street-lamps will turn on.
We will walk back to our house. But if I were to remain
outside, alone, in another life, then, looking up,
I might wish to erase ram, archer, horse,
see things simply as they are — small piercing stars
in the immense, immeasurable dark.

Jessica Martinez

# TRANSITIONS

I watch my life
being neatly packed
into moving boxes
then into a shipping container
and finally sealed.
I sigh
and sign all the documents
that an overseas move demands.

At our new destination
we camp in our living room
and imagine how all of our furniture
crosses the Atlantic on an unknown vessel.

I meet neighbors, open bank accounts,
buy cars, health insurance, phone contracts
and get tired of our improvised life.

Then comes delivery day
with glass tables scratched,
other minor defects
and a house full of boxes
to unpack.

I am exhausted
yet I know this was the easy part.
Settling in, making friends,
arriving properly
takes time.

I will lose count of
the faux pas we will make,
the irritated faces trying to understand our accents,
our google searches of 'how to' and 'what to,'
the moments in which we don't understand,
the moments in which they don't understand
and judge and draw conclusions.
I will stop counting
the times we feel inadequate
and so very different,
the moments of embarrassment we will go through

because we did not know any better.
Our daughter will be the only girl
in her first school picture
who does not wear a dress
because we do not know unwritten rules.
We know so little
but each time we learn.

Almost every step brings new wisdom
as we balance between two lives.
Gradually the mass of strangers
that occupy the restaurant tables around us
will be replaced by familiar faces
and I will patiently wait for the day
that someone greets me
in the grocery store.
My ears will smile
as I hear my name,
I will turn around
and we will chat
as if we have always belonged here.

Jennifer Brooke

## BLENDED FAMILY

Things like sofas and chairs we bought new
Rugs too—except for that old sisal runner
I nailed to the stairs so the kids wouldn't slip

We spent $500 on a vintage velvet wingback
We tried in three spots before returning
The long brown hard couch was also probably
A mistake but we made it work

Things we had doubles of we simply used both
Chef's knives, wine glasses, dessert plates, cereal bowls
What didn't mix and match we alternated

Only the cutlery jumbled together
Thrown in a too-small drawer, spoons and forks so
Mismatched they refused to nest one atop another and
Tangled and tumbled and scratched instead

We used it all, sitting on this and sipping from that
And laughing and living and pretending
We were cereal bowls and probably knowing we were cutlery

Kate Falvey

## GINGERBREAD MIX

So this year, penitent, I
bought a mix.
The requisite men were cut
and baked and
it all took under an hour, even
with waiting
for the rounds of dough
to chill. What is it with this
need to spice the air
with nutmeg, cinnamon, and dark
disavowal? Where is the reproof
and where the violation
of the old wives' from-scratch code?

Last year, the house fell down.
Gumdrops popped with seismic
imbecility and a farcical music-hall patter
held up my nerve. Something about
effort unwasted and
still being tasty and
togetherness being
the durable goal.
I could have bludgeoned
the idiot thing, its licorice shutters and
hedgerows of toffee
too garish and ambitious
for a simple bungalow.
Icing thick as avalanches – a
mountain resort's worth –
on the eaves.
Nothing would hold. Nothing
would withstand my clumsy
eagerness to please.
As if houses of cookies
could trump
houses of cards.

Pound cake, angel food, puddings, meringues, and
breads with a hint of cardamom –
there is, in my hurried resurrection of
kitchens of yore,

the fairy dust of sifted flour,
oleo and oats, the crisp dither of brown
sugar rasping golden oaths,
the whir of my mother's mixer,
the rim of a ceaseless day,
the untrammeled joy of licking
the bright and mystic blades.

Kimberly Weikert

## LABOR PAINS

It is said that "Time stops for no man."
But it does for women.

The flood stopped my mother in her tracks.
With a child on each hip and
a basket of laundry she crossed the
river water on her doorstep.

Women know there is always work
to be undone and then done again.
Weeks, and months, and years
of the same day's work.

Today we will arrive at the
same place we were yesterday
and meet there again tomorrow.
And I will be changed into nothing new.

## THE BUILDER

Long past eight in South L.A.,
Vanessa feeds her key into the lock,
her brain still vibrating from three hours on the freeway,
tries to shake loose dirt that has a strangle hold
on her red braids, has taken up residence beneath her nails,
carefully removes boots camouflaged in mud,
laces fraying at the edges.


The boy remembers grits
now cold, milk that has run out,
the hollow house after school,
hours waiting for the creak of the front door.
He does not answer her hello,
stands stiff in her arms, says
*Mama, change your clothes.*


She weathers his words
like so many on the job –
coworkers' propositions, dress-downs
by white bosses with clipboards, as she shoulders
sand bags, steel beams,
pays no mind to wet cement
that weeps on her overalls.


She surveys the kitchen,
sees past crumbs, scorched pots,
the crack in the window,
to the day her boy will go to college,
and she will welcome to the job
other hard-hat sisters breaking ground
for their sons.


*For Vanessa, a pioneer of the L.A. Black Workers' Center*

## DIVESTITURE

It needed deep focus,
a kind of séance,
to recall the dinner
that I cooked last night.
This mattered, the way
communing with the dead
matters to some. Finally
my mind's eye
saw through the murk:
orange carrots,
green and white bok choi—
a skein I could trace
to sautéed chicken pieces.
The retrieval such a relief.
Seventy-five years
of quotidian clutter,
the brain needs a drain pipe
to make room for daily accretion.

The house too, needs a purge.
Winnow the shelves
of books not enticing enough
to reread, and those past charity—
their dry, yellow pages
en route to dust.
Shred records-- transactions
that held together
the skeleton of a life.
Pack up blouses
faded or passé, skirts
too long, too short, high heels
languishing in boxes.
Down the chute—grieving—
throw dog-eared hiking books,
trail maps tearing at the folds,
boots that gripped steep rising paths.

When they find me
there will be no clutter:
books I saved
and was reading
as if for the first time.

Carol Levin

## NOW THAT THE NEST IS EMPTY

Stalking the streets
in search of music
and human spectacle
under New Orleans' French filigree
you catch that *cooly-cool boy*
whose brass bell
flares soprano
jazz.

All five-foot-two of you
celebrates
the horn that gleams
your gray eyes into moons.
A familiar gesture
lengthens your neck,
not quite the curve
of a trumpeter swan.

From the daily
commute, from workaday
Greenwich Village, from
single mother-fussing over
only child, from the five-floor
walk-up over the falafel place:
here to bloodbrown
bouillabaisse and Cajun soul.

Tongue catches
the last sugar of a sweet
beignet. Without looking up
you glide moltenwhite
arms through
and button on
your new persona.
Now you name
the new you, *Lone Wolf*

Katherine Durham Oldmixon

## POST HASTE

I never miss my period.
The last time I remember
seeing it was in Japan,

a tsunami on a train, not
sitting for fear it would
out me. Of course it had

gone missing before—four times,
but then the absence
meant something present.

This time, after the floods,
it just slipped away, like
afterbirth or childhood,

like albumin pouring through
my fingers when I separate
it from the yolk in my palm.

I imagine I am pregnant
with time, my blood coursing
in my sons and daughters,

in my grandbabies. I suppose
my body fills and empties still.
But it is with the whole night sky.

Judith Waller Carroll

## EMPTY NEST

It takes so little
to make the dog happy—
her pill ground with chicken,
an extra biscuit.

How smoothly we've shifted
our need to nurture:
my patience with the cat's
rough tongue on my cheek,
his need to be carried,

the doting way you spoon
peanut butter mixture
into the log feeder,
scatter safflower seeds
for the cardinals
no matter the weather,

how delighted we are
that the woodpecker's back,
how we celebrate
by mixing more suet.

# ASSAYING

How can I assess whether we're thriving here?
The cactus blooms, prolific candelabra of blossom.
The jade plant which almost died when we moved
in is studded with small eruptions of new growth.
The new orchid that was so beautiful is bare now.
My mother-in-law's old clock runs perfectly.

The broken day fills with pale creamy light. Do
I want a plant in the study? If I put blue glass
bottles on a windowsill would they catch the light?
Would the dogs knock them down? No and yes,
I fear. How can I learn to allow: the weather,
the dogs, the changes? Yesterday I do the first

real gardening here: weed beds in front of
the house, plant bulbs: hyacinth, daffodil,
crocus—the hyacinth in a row, the daffodils
in clusters, the crocus scattered. All the lists
become a life list: not sightings but sitings,
insights, what we're called to, called for:

what we must learn, serve, voice. Yesterday
I realize that one reason I don't understand
why my son is glad to have us living here is
that when I was his age my parents had both
been dead for decades. I am not too old to
learn—if I allow it. This morning, I choose

to allow it. I'm happy. Happy even though
I know I could die before spring, die before
seeing the crocus, daffodil, hyacinth bloom
for the first time. Wilfully, I assess this here,
this now, and choose to call it happiness:
my body alive in this house, garden, life.

Patrice Boyer Claeys

## MOTHER'S TRIP TO RED LOBSTER TWO WEEKS AFTER MOVING TO A RETIREMENT HOME

After decades scoffing at *old people,* their plodding,
grouchy refusals, confused repetition, fingers that don't
unfold, purses that don't snap, shopping carts blocking
the aisles, bent over coupons they can't see; after years
of fear disguised as disdain and false assertions—"I'd rather *kill*
myself than go to a place like that,"—she finds herself
a member of the last sorority, communal group of humans
hunched toward their own demise, surprised at how easy it is
to quiet the habits of a life when the time comes.  She allows
the perky social director to lead her and eight stout souls
with walkers, sturdy shoes and shaky hands to the van
which lifts them magically, pneumatically, so much folding
metal, arms and legs that roll and hold this teetering frailty
behind bars.  Off they go, chattering praise for the late
November cornfields, welcome expanses of open space.
They clutch hankies, thank the sun, so weak as it fails
to outrun winter, for every bit of warmth they hold in spotted
ropy hands.  They arrive and disembark.  Everyone caught up
in so much doing:  the mall's wide halls, elevators that mercifully
reduce stairs to the push of a button (if only it's the right one).
She has ventured forth, added her name, entered the flow.
She raises her glass, heavy and red with liquid beads pearling
the surface, tears the bread, steadies the little Neptune fork,
spears the shrimp, and licks the slick shimmer with her tongue.

## A BRAIDED TALE

### First Love

First love is best.

First kiss, rooted in hunger.

First soft-as-an-eyelash touch, fingers reaching for nothing more than what's within their reach. She begins with her mother's mouth, makes her way to random strands of hair tickling her face.

Candy, not Candice, is her name. You don't have to be a witch in a gingerbread house to be tempted by scrumptious fingers, jelly toes. You do have to be a mother to lose yourself in the powdery charm, the soft tickle of downy hair the color of sand.

Every day, every week brings something new. A smile that knows something beyond pleasure. A hug that knows what it means to feel safe.

A word. *Mama.*

Baby steps are the bravest, even if they take time. Big leaps take some hedging, even if they bank on trust. Fall down. Get up.

Run Candy Run.

### If I Have One Life to Live . . .

Edna Gottlieb, a new client, comes in the other day. "I hear you do magic with red," she says. She's fifty-four, tired of dirty blonde.

I run my fingers through her hair, the color and texture of straw, remind her there's nothing really 'dirty' about blonde. Not that I don't owe my livelihood to those mad men who make the mirror spin words, the hint of a mouse running through brown, the grit of dirt squeezing the vibrancy from blonde. I show her a picture, my daughter, a little pipsqueak at the time, her hair reeking from tar soap, tears streaming down her face. Janice (*Janeese*, as she was known), already a mean girl at seven, tells Candy her hair is always dirty. Blonde. Gives her some 'special' soap to take the dirt out. Not my daughter's proudest moment. I show Edna another photo of Candy, my sweet girl, all grown up, ombré waves cascading past her shoulders. Ironic, don't you think? Edna points to a snapshot on my mirror, Rosanne D'Amico. A client looking for that one-life-to-live Clairol promise when she first came to me years ago. A little coaxing and I convince her she'll look washed out as a blonde. A little chemistry and I turn her into the redhead she was meant to be. Yesterday, after months away, she comes in, clumps of hair dotting her scalp like haystacks, in need of something I was not prepared to give. She hands me a wig, the color not quite right, her eyes shadowed and pleading.

"I'll see what I can do," I say.

## Lost Love

I have my mother's hands and my father's feet. He taught me the art of walking barefoot, never a stubbed toe. She taught me to roll dough into stars, twist my own hair into a perfect French braid. I keep it short these days.

She gave up mixing colors on a canvas (no career in that) for the chemistry of highlights and hair dye. Could put a client into a trance with her delicate brush strokes.

He became a track coach, taught me all about stride and spring. Tension and release. One foot a bow, the other an arrow.

If I spread my hands on a table you would see the gentle curve of my pinkies. Parentheses letting you in on a secret, that heart line of mine (hers), inherited. It worries me.

Pedicurists always remark on my long, straight toes. Just like my father's, I never tell them.

He walked—no ran—out on us the day after high school graduation. Two men came looking for him a few days later. One coughed with each drag of his cigarette, gave my mother a matchbook with a phone number on it. *You hear from him make sure he calls*. The other left a trail of cologne.

My mother used to take it in stride, my flitting around—city to city, no place ever quite right to roost—even if she thought I couldn't stay put because I was looking for my father. Then she got sick, irritable all the time. Now she says (between fits of coughing), *enough with the nothing-as-constant-as-change bullshit. There are only two constants in life: you're born; you die.*

These days I'm in Seattle. I run a bakery.

My father just shows up one day, tells me I'm a hard person to track down.

"Look who's talking."

"What's with the blue hair?" he asks.

"What's with the long ponytail?" Fifteen years since I last saw him and already gray.

He looks around, customers crowding the counter. Star-shaped vanilla snaps are my specialty.

"Spoke to your mother last week." He looks over his shoulder, the air of a man still feeling hunted. His hiking boots are old, worn out.

"So?" I imagine the shock to her system, his voice so out of the blue.

He picks at his teeth with his thumbnail. Shakes his head. "Who could know a hello would become a good-bye?"

I hand him a cookie, it melts in his mouth. "Just like your mother's—even better."

I open the door, ask him to leave. "The way you change a recipe is the secret to making it yours."

Sarah Kennedy

# OCCUPYING MOTHERHOOD

A few weeks ago, I received a script outlining a new patient I'll pretend to be during practice sessions with medical students. I'm helping train the students in empathetic presentation of bad news. They're making their mistakes with me, a medical actor, because I won't be traumatized by callousness in the ominous figure in the white coat if we're both pretending.

Jean Smith has two daughters, though it's her youngest, Olivia, who is relevant to the case. The medical students are evaluated on whether or not they can get Jean to consider a feeding tube for Olivia, who Jeans brings into the emergency room malnourished for the fourth time in the past six months. A disease in infancy left Olivia with developmental delays, and she is a fussy baby, especially during meal times. Jean feeds Olivia homemade purees with a syringe. She kneels next to Olivia's high chair for an hour at every meal and 45 minutes for snacks. Still, Olivia isn't getting all the nutrients she needs, and the doctors in the emergency room have pushed the idea of a feeding tube every night Jean has spent in a plastic chair, Olivia sleeping tangled in IV lines. Jean is resistant — Olivia would have to undergo surgery to have the tube placed. And what about all the afternoons Jean spent with a worn copy of *Meals for Meeting Toddler Milestones* lain directly underneath the high chair, flipping pages with her knee while she coaxed Olivia to open her mouth for even just a few syringes of the puree? The doctors tell Jean she can be replaced by a tube. Jean worries she has failed as a mother.

"You have amazing dedication," a medical student gushes, her hand on my knee. I want to tell her I had to look up what exactly a puree was. She knows I'm an actor, and she's acting just as much as I am, but we're both caught up in the image of Jean on the kitchen floor with a syringe; Jean at the grocery store telling her older daughter to put back the fruit snacks because organic produce is expensive; Jean trying to be grateful her second child lived through that early illness at all.

The sessions with medical students are short, maybe 15 minutes. We stop for feedback and talk about how important it is for medical professionals to consider the feelings of the family when doling out gastrostomy tubes. Jean's tears still in my eyes, I tell the students what might seem like an easy solution to them is a monumental event to the people their decisions will affect. Between sessions, I sit on a bench outside the meeting room we're using for the simulation exercise. By cruel design, the room is on the border of the children's hospital cafeteria, where real parents with purple darkness below their eyes like the eye shadow mockery I have under mine eat droopy grilled cheeses and don't speak. I try not to look up at the nurses eating together, the parents holding hands over lunch trays, the siblings with coloring books and juice boxes. I'm an imposter with a notecard. I get to memorize what they have to live.

Practice patients like me are necessary, of course, and useful — medical students fumble with us, the lucky ones without intubated children, so they don't hurt anyone really going through what we are paid to inhabit. But I'm keenly aware of how exploitative this line of work necessarily is when the reality of what I'm helping prepare these medical students for is in front of me. I want to apologize for who I'm not to any individual in the cafeteria who believes I'm the young mom I purport to be. I'm filled with the empathy I'm looking for in the medical students.

The facilitators for this session ask me to give feedback in character to sustain suspension of disbelief for the students. This is unusual — we typically give feedback as actors, as ourselves — so I mention it to a co-worker next time I work. "But you're not a mother," she tells me, startled. "You can't give that kind of feedback. You don't know how you'd react unless you live it." She's a mother. I tell her truthfully that I'm sorry in an attempt to atone.

I memorize statements but fixate on Jean. Does she feel guilty for wanting an easier baby? Is she ungrateful for not appreciating what she has? For one of my other cases, the medical students have to tell me my newborn is brain dead. That might be another woman's reality in the room next door to Jean. Neither is my reality. But if that changes, I hope the doctor who reads the outline of that case to me has practiced.

Therese Gilardi

## CHANGE OF LIVES

I loathe letting go of my children because I don't want to grow up. For decades I've enjoyed using motherhood as a personally and culturally acceptable rationale for failing to develop my own independent adult identity. Motherhood has been my evergreen excuse, the ultimate trump card I play whenever I'm called upon to take responsibility for myself. But now my children have blown me a kiss, packed a U-Haul, and moved into a tomorrow I can never inhabit, leaving me bitter and broken.

You're appalled and I don't blame you. We're well into the twenty-first century and I am a woman who has never lived in a time when "The Feminine Mystique" was not in print. I've spent my life in the U.S. and Western Europe, surrounded by women who have held enormous political, social and economic power while also grasping the hands of their sons and daughters. I am not from a religious or ethnic background that endorses the restrictive bonds I've put on myself. I have no excuse for my years of using motherhood as a means of escaping the adult world. All I have is an explanation, an ugly truth I have only recently begun to admit to myself.

I didn't mean for this to happen, for "Mommy" to be the only way in which I defined myself. I never intended for decades to pass without outside employment or relationships independent of my roles as mother and, less importantly, wife. Growing up I was the girl who hated dolls and babysitting. I preferred climbing trees and dreaming of the day when I'd live in a far-off sophisticated city and work as a foreign correspondent. But then I met a man and the script changed. He was strong-willed, obsessive in his desire to quiet his own demons, and I was far too weak. Rather quickly I began to abandon myself, until there was nothing left but a fertile shell. Painful as it is to admit, I saw motherhood as the way out of my invisibility.

71

My babies were my lifeboat, my sole reason to climb out of my despair. I couldn't live for myself but I could live for my son and daughter. And that's what I did, for virtually my entire adult life. I lived in places I despised, neglected social as well as professional opportunities lest they inconvenience my kids, and stayed in a marriage my husband and I both agree was wretched. But like all self-proclaimed martyrs I did not act selflessly. No, I took a lot of pride in my "sacrifice." And of course I was relieved. After all I had one of the few socially acceptable reasons for being perpetually housebound.

Now don't get me wrong. I was not a lay-about. And I am not saying raising children doesn't require commitment and responsibility, which are of course two of the hallmarks of maturity. Rather I am referring to my continued habitation in the world of the nursery long after my children became engaged in their own lives. I'm talking about all those hours, days, weeks, months, years that I forfeited while my children were at school. This was time I could have used to develop my own skills. But I'd forgotten how to think for myself. It had been so long and the notion was so uncomfortable. It was much easier to wrap myself in the cloak of motherhood, so soothing to double down on my maternal devotion and bury myself in the comforting world of the playground.

The first time I heard the word codependent I knew it described me. I saw that my behavior was less than admirable, that in many ways it was counter to the goal of mothering, which is to turn out independent offspring. This awareness did not, however, motivate me to change. Instead it led to a desire to cling even tighter to my role as Mum.

But then it all changed. The children graduated. They moved on. They moved out. And I was left with nothing but the mounds of photos I'd taken, documentary evidence of how I'd spent my adult years, a husband I didn't know, and the crushing grief-laced knowledge that I had never lived for myself. My yesterdays were gone and the number of my tomorrows had dwindled.

That's where I am now, standing on the flashpoint between the past and the future, wondering how to build a present. Although of course I will always be Mother, my children no longer need me, at least not in the way they used to. I've been made redundant and there's no unemployment package, no career counseling, not even a gold watch to compensate me for my years of faithful service. Life is forcing me to change. I must finally stand on my own and claim a place for myself. I have no choice. I can no longer use motherhood as an excuse for the comment that appeared most often on my childhood report cards: "Did not live up to her potential."

## THE COCKTAIL DRESS

I dreaded telling my mother that I had split up with my second husband.   When we married two years ago she was thrilled.  She went though her address book calling family and friends telling everyone how happy she was that her daughter, a "gay divorcee" for twenty–five years, had finally found someone she loved and was settling down. As a result of her calls my new husband and I received many congratulatory cards with enclosed checks totaling two thousand dollars.

I forced myself to get on the phone to Maryland where my parents lived to break the news. My mother did know we were having problems, but I had never told her in detail about Steven's constant pot smoking or his increasing jealousy and possessiveness. He wanted to go everywhere with me, even to the gynecologist. He wanted to be with me in the examining room.

My mother listened in silence. After I told her I had filed for divorce, she gave a big sigh. "Next time don't marry someone you only know for three months," she said and hung up the phone.

My parents came to visit me three weeks later, bringing a dress my mother made for me. "I made you this cocktail dress to wear to parties," she said. She was a superb seamstress with a flourishing alterations business. The dress was of fine silk velvet, sunset red, and strapless. It reached to my ankles with long slits on each side because, as my mother told me, "you were so lucky to inherit my legs."

The fit was perfect. She had tailored it to herself, she and I being the same size. "You look like a movie star," she said. "You wear this dress when you go out to cocktail parties and special occasions, you'll meet someone special, someone good enough for you."

The dress was gorgeous. I wore it to all sorts of parties, art openings and three weddings. I wore it to many poetry readings and always wore it when I hosted the yearly Bukowski tribute evenings at the Bowery Poetry Club.

Seven Bukowski tribute evenings later I still hadn't met that special someone, although I did have an initially promising affair with a skinny Irish actor I met when I had it on. One morning at 3 a.m. I woke from our bed of love to see him coming out of the bathroom wearing it.

On my mother's seventy-fifth birthday I went down to Maryland so the whole family could celebrate together.  I brought her a marble cheesecake, her favorite, from Juniors. My brother brought cold cuts from the famous Chick and Ruth Deli in Annapolis over to my parents' house because my mother and I were wild for their corned beef sandwiches. After the meal and the candles and cake, my father, brother, his wife and his two kids went into the living room to watch Seinfeld re-runs.

My mother and I went into the kitchen to load the dishes in the dishwasher. When we were done, she took me by the hand and led me to sit opposite her at the kitchen table. "I need to talk to you," she said.

"You're over sixty now, your looks may go soon.  It will be harder for you to meet someone.  Seven years already that you're divorced. There's no one to care for you, what happens if you get sick? You're not trying hard enough to meet someone, you need to go out more, need to…."

I interrupted her, "I don't believe in 'trying' to meet someone. I can't live my life trying to meet someone. I'm the one responsible for my happiness, no one else."

"What's wrong with having someone help you with your happiness? Are you too proud to accept help?" she cut in. "It's not good, not healthy, you all the time alone." Her litany was upsetting me, in part because I was starting to have some of the same thoughts myself.

"Ma," I cut in, my voice rising sharply despite my efforts to control it, "What difference does it make?" I asked her. "You're born alone and you die alone."

My mother drew back as if I had slapped her. She sat up very straight. She looked me straight in the eyes. "What happened to your brain? How can you say that? You weren't born alone, I was with you," she said, piercing me to the heart.

I was so ashamed. I felt tears welling up. "You're right, ma," I managed to mumble.

"Your mother is always right," she answered.

She died two years later. It is seventeen years now she is gone. Since her death I think of her every day. Knowing how much she loved me has gotten me through some tough times.

I still wear the cocktail dress. I will cherish it always. It hangs in the front of my closet so I can see it whenever I open the door.

Lorraine Currelley

## TANGO

Her nightly ritual began with her bath. Slowly pouring the perfumed liquid into the tub filling with water. The sweet smelling fragrance of her bath oils always gave her pleasure. Not the pleasure she remembered with past lovers, but pleasure all the same. She stood before the mirror watching as her bathrobe slipped to the floor, falling around her ankles. Admiring her image, she stood in the mirror allowing her eyes and fingertips to explore each part of her body. She had not changed much over the years. Looking back at her was a very attractive woman with a slight protruding belly, fuller hips and breasts, graying hair and a few wrinkles. She felt good and beautiful. She did not shrink from age but welcomed it. She caressed the water gently, picking up a hand full of bubbles. Resting her head against the inflated bath pillow, she closed her eyes slowly and took a deep breath losing herself in her thoughts.

Before tango she spent countless hours at home dancing alone. She often wondered how many men and women were leading themselves across their private dance floors. How many burying their sensuality and sexuality? She refused to listen to the ads for creams promising to restore youth peddled by the young to the old. Sexist and ageist attempts to convince those of her generation they had outlived their worth. Ads promising if their products were used they could turn back the hands of time. She sunk deeper into the water, allowing memories of passionate nights filled with lovemaking and tender words shared between lovers fill her. Thoughts of heaving breasts, gyrating hips, feet and legs circling the floor as they once did the backs of hungry and demanding lovers. Men and women hiding desire, need and loneliness. Tango meant and restored passion. Tango meant life. Tango meant magic.

She remembered reading an ad one morning in the community events section of the local newspaper. The ad was for free tango lessons in the park on Saturdays. At first, she dismissed the ad by turning the page. Later that evening at home she found herself thinking about it. It's a silly idea. After much thought she made a decision to attend purely out of curiosity as an observer. Besides, who knows, it might turn out to be fun. She arrived early at the park and sat on a bench within full viewing of the designated dance area. She was greeted warmly, eyed with curiosity and asked if she came to participate by other persons seated in the same area. Smiling politely, she replied she was an observer. She watched males and females of all ethnicities, cultures, ages, shapes, sizes and heights arriving for the afternoon's festivities. Some were dressed dramatically in what appeared to be| costumes. There were others who walked with the posture and grace of professional dancers. Heads held erect and focused. They reminded her of those dance competitions public television broadcasted. There was an air of expectation in the faces of both participants and observers. Sensing something special was about to take place, her heart beat fast.

Dancers were divided into three groups, beginner, intermediate and professional. Beginners received basic instruction and intermediates were instructed in a dance routine. Professionals had the option of joining intermediates or enjoying an afternoon of dancing. Sometimes, the professionals would assist with the instruction of beginners. Once the music started the park as if by magic was suddenly transformed into a ballroom. A room of vivid colors and bodies floating across the floor. She marveled at the joy, excitement and total abandon of the dancers. Everyone found themselves caught up in tango's magic. Her body swayed, aching to give itself. She knew she would return; only next week she would find herself in tango's arms. She left singing joyfully and exchanging greetings with everyone she met and neighbors from her community.

She became a familiar face on the dance floor. The smooth material of her dress flowing freely against her velvety skin as she moved. Her legs complimented by the heels she wore to dance in. In the arms of tango she existed in a world of sensuality and passion. Tango was memory, magic and freedom. She was no longer invisible and merely existing. Buried beneath her skin, the woman she knew herself to be appeared for all to see. She was vibrant and alive. Each week she filled with excitement thinking of her tango. She found herself preparing the same way as she had prepared for evenings with lovers. Tango's intimacy and passion made remaining strangers an impossibility. Everyone was united in this great love. Imagine intergenerational couples dancing as though lovers; this was the nature of tango. Everyone disappearing into the dance.

On arriving at the park she changed into her dance shoes, took a deep breath, exhaled and smiled. She was suddenly swept up into the arms of one of the regulars. The material of her dress swayed and clung to her body, like a possessive lover. Theirs was a partnering of movement and grace. She matched his movements with her own. Both gliding across the floor as though one body. Both uninhibited in their joy. She felt his hot breathe against her cheek. They were both seduced by its power. His hand caressing the small of her back as he led her across the dance floor. There was never a need to explain the fire burning beneath their skin and passion. Tango was a delicious and demanding lover. One not easily satisfied. One you gave your all.

## UNPACKING

I've moved to a town where the women look like me. Short, with curly hair, strong legs and anxious expressions inherited from grandmothers who fretted about hungry children, Sabbath challah, invading Cossacks. My new kinswomen worry about what's for dinner, waiting on carpool lines, helping with homework. I've come home, returned to my tribe.

--

As I unpack I find my mother's wedding china, gold-rimmed, cream-colored Minton bordered with blue and rose flower petals. My mother and I traded wedding sets many years ago. When I became engaged I told her I didn't want a registry, fine china and good silver, but my mother insisted, encouraging me to choose a Fitz and Floyd gold and white contemporary pattern. She cared about setting a nice table—ironic, since she hated to cook. She did enjoy entertaining friends and family with coffee and cake. Known for traveling to bakeries all over the county and across state lines, she searched for the best pastries, travelling to Pakula's in Teaneck for rugellach, The Runcible Spoon in Nyack for sachertorte, Sugar Flake in Wyckoff for cookies. People thought she was crazy—who would care so much about dessert—but she enjoyed these excursions, returning home and arranging elaborate platters mounded with desserts. On my Fitz and Floyd china.

I look at the Minton, delicate, fragile, out of date, and I'm glad to have it because it was hers. I wonder who I will pass it on to and can think of no one. My sons are with young women who will probably inherit their mother's or grandmother's china. For the time being, the Minton is mine.

--

My husband studies the cascade of crystals dangling from the chandelier in our new kitchen. "What happened to you?" he asks. "You like this? You used to want simplicity, understatement. This place looks like the Crystal Palace."

"I've changed," I say.

My husband looks at me in astonishment. "Who are you?" he asks.

"Change is good," I say, but I can tell he doesn't believe me.

--

Our new home is for grown ups. No navy and white striped wallpaper with a racing car border, no red and white checked paper bordered by little-boy trains. Gone are the Beanie Babies, baseball trophies, bobblehead dolls, even the books: *Where the Wild Things Are, Frog and Toad*, the complete set of Harry Potter. For many years I couldn't get rid of my kids' things, not when they left to go to college, not when they graduated. And then suddenly I went on a cleaning rampage because we were moving. Books were donated to the library, blue jeans and flannel shirts went to Goodwill, stuff ended up in the garbage. My younger son was philosophical. "I don't need it anyway," he said. My older son was sentimental. "I can't revisit this. Do whatever you have to with my things."

In the end, I did.

I also gave away my vintage salt-and-pepper shakers, ceramic teapots, costume jewelry from the past 20 years.

My mother was a collector, too; she favored Limoges teacups.

When my firstborn was 16 months old, my husband and I relocated from upstate New York to New Jersey. My husband's new job began before we could close on our house, and, with no place to live, we moved in with my parents. My mother refused to childproof, believing it was never too early to teach discipline and self-control. So for nine weeks, nine very long weeks, I followed my toddler son around the house, removing his restless, inquisitive fingers from the vast array of porcelain teacups that filled the living room. One day he accidentally cracked the glass inset in my mother's French provincial coffee table, but instead of telling her about it and offering to pay, I covered the crack with some of her books. I suppose it was revenge for my mother's refusal to accommodate and make the house more child-friendly. On the other hand, I never asked her if the three of us could move in. I needed a place to live, and I told her I would be coming home with my child and husband. I never thought to ask.

--

Pandora, the first woman, was given the gift of a beautiful box, which she opened, not knowing she would release evil into the world.

At the bottom of her box there was something that remained, something that would guide us in the darkness.

Hope. Hope was what remained.

**Heather Haldeman**

# MOVING ON

My eighty-eight-year-old mother's eyes widened with childish glee when the male nurse entered the hospital room. She beamed as he lifted her wrist to check her vitals. Mom slipped her foot out from under the thin cotton blanket.

"Want to see my tattoo?" she asked him. "It's right here on my ankle. Got it three years ago."

With my mother, it's always been all about the men. What I didn't know about my mother was that she embraced change. "I'm adaptable," she told me after her third move— assisted care facility, rehab facility, another assisted living facility—in as many weeks after her hospital stay. "It's a talent. Like being a good singer." She paused. "And, resilience. You have to be born with it."

For years, my mother had begged to stay in her home in Bel Air rather than move to an assisted living facility. But her balance was getting worse with her Parkinson's and she agreed to make the move a year ago. The first day in assisted living, she asked us why we hadn't brought her there sooner. "I love all the action. The people. And, of course, the men. It didn't take long for her to find one. "The doctor," she told me with a suspicious gleam in her eye.

"Already?" I asked.

"His wife's upstairs on the third floor with Alzheimer's. She'll never know."

"So, how do you know this doctor has a thing for you, Mom?"

"We share pickles on our plates at lunch."

"I don't get it," my sister, April, said. " I mean, at her age, isn't she over all this finding-a-man stuff?"

But then, after nearly a full year in assisted living, she fell. She was lucky - no injury – but that didn't stop her from sneaking around without using her walker. "I'll look old using it," she told me.

"Mom, you *are* old!"

The second fall came a week later. This time, landing her in the hospital. A bump on the head. After the thankfully clean CAT scan, she understood the risk. "I dodged a bullet," she said. "I get it now that I'm in a wheelchair."

When the hospital released her to a Rehabilitation Health Center, my friend Wendy sighed. "She may not like this. These places can be so depressing."

Mom proved her wrong. Two days in, Edith, her roommate became her "new best friend." Even when Edith went home, Mom adapted to the next roommate even though she was "a screamer."

"It's not a problem. I just told her to shut up," Mom said.

And then, there was Joseph…her male physical therapist. "His muscles are the size of Guam. A real looker, that one."

"I can't believe I'm glad that I fell," Mom admitted. "I've moved on. I like working out in the rehab room every day, and I like the people here. I met some woman from Omaha today. She likes flowers and all that crap. Total opposite of me. I told her that I was married three times. That's my claim to fame, you know."

"What about the activities?"

"I do everything," she replied. "I even Bible Study. Bor-ring! They just went on about Aaron and the weeds…"

After three weeks, Mom was set to return to her assisted living. This time, however, the social worker at the Rehab mandated that she move from her regular room to the third floor, the "Reminiscence Floor."

"Why?" I asked.

"Your mother only scored 13 out of 29 on the dementia test. She has trouble remembering things."

"What eighty-eight year old doesn't?" I spoke to the director at her assisted living.

"She's a fall risk, too," he told me. It was clear a few days after she moved that this was *not* the right place for Mom. She was still with-it and needed to be surrounded by others like her, people with some spunk.

Seven days later, a bed opened in The Jewish Home for the Aging, a skilled nursing facility renown for its excellent care. I'd been in contact with them, just waiting for an opening—but would she like it?

The morning of the move, April and I swooped in. Packed her up. Wheelchair in the trunk and Mom was off to another new life. "Trust me, Mom. Have I ever let you down?"

"Nope," she said on the way over. "It was tough," she admitted, "being on that third floor. The crazies got to me. I ate alone."

After a twenty-minute drive, I pulled into the Jewish Home.

"Holy Christ," she said. "This looks like Paramount Studio."

I couldn't have asked for a better reaction.

Two days in, I came to visit. At noon, I wheeled her into the dining room. "Right here," she said. "This is where I sit."

I rolled her up to her place at the table. "Meet Bernie," she said to a man on her right. "And this is Ruth. She's a hundred and four!" Ruth gave me a cute wave.

I said my goodbyes, but my mother had already moved on. "Bernie, do you like pickles?"

Marion Deutsche Cohen

## THE NURSING TODDLER LEARNS ABOUT LIFE

He used to say "I wanna eat so I feel better" and "I feel better." Now he sometimes says "I don't feel better now. I don't feel better from eating."

He used to say "I don't like that side. I want the other side." Now he sometimes says "The other side's gonna be just like that side. Both sides are the same."

Pam Bernard

## THE GIFT

Knowing Mrs. Gildersleeve suffered in extreme heat, my mother had phoned and, when there was no answer, stopped by. *I'm here, Anna,* Mother said softly, then pulled a chair close. Mrs. Gildersleeve lay on her flowered divan, the pink and yellow roses on her flowered dress wilting onto her generous body. Her startlingly pale face floated in a sea of leaves and trailing blossoms covering the wallpaper and carpet. Even the drapes were flowered.

She had been an ambassador's wife, and an opera singer. On the mantle was a photograph of her next to Winston Churchill. She was taller, with broad shoulders and a confident smile. A large woman herself, Mother for once seemed oddly small, settled in beside her.

This was a time when experience and intuition accounted for something. One could be a practical nurse with no formal education, and my mother's reputation as a caring companion was well known, even among the wealthy tenants of the Griswold House, like Mrs. Gildersleeve.

People would call at all hours asking for Mother's advice, or for her to come right away. If she were cooking dinner, she'd call my sisters and me into the kitchen and quietly explain what to do to get the meal on the table. Then off she'd go. That day she had tried everything to make our neighbor comfortable, removing her nylon hose and loosening her corset. But nothing had worked.

Mother had lived through much, and her face held all that anguish and heartbreak, but a measure of joy, too, so that when a rare smile occasioned her lips, her eyes remained dark and sad. But she knew how to feed ten of us around the table by stretching the small portion of meat she could afford with potatoes, or by serving biscuits and gravy or chipped beef on toast. But if you weren't feeling well, you wanted Esther there, sitting by you, fixing milk toast if you needed nourishment.

Now Mrs. Gildersleeve lay prostrate in the stifling heat. Her breath had slowed to a fluttery gurgle, her lower jaw working with each inhale and exhale. Mother took a deep breath as if trying to help her, shifting slightly in the straight-backed chair. She turned then and gazed intently at me. I often accompanied her on these visits, cherishing our few times alone. I would be eleven on my next birthday, and because I was wandering in those middle years between being a child and no longer a child, when the world was full of mysterious signs with few words attached, I sensed something was terribly wrong.

Then Mother held forth as if she had been given the gift of speech for the first time.

*That spring was a wet one and by morning the draw was bank full,* she said suddenly, her voice clear and bright. *By afternoon the Pumpkin had flooded half way to the barn.*

Mrs. Gildersleeve's hand moved imperceptibly. Mother took it in hers and continued.

*Sheep don't like to get their feet wet, so my brother William and I laid cornstalks in their stall in case the creek kept on coming.* She was almost chanting now. *But we'd no sooner finished when the barn door flapped open and a tremendous rush of water came in.*

I sat dumbfounded. My mother had never once told me a story of any kind, certainly never opened her childhood to me. When I'd asked what it was like when she was young, she'd say she lived it once and didn't ever care to return. But there I was with her, a girl my age, I imagined, water closing in on us, in a place more vivid than my own life—the acrid, almost pleasant smell of the barn, the sheep, bleating pitifully, heavy with wool. Shearing had been planned for that week. Taken by the water the sheep would surely drown.

And so it went that day attending Mrs. Gildersleeve, my mother pitched headlong into memory long buried, into a swelling stream gone mad, each of us on the fragile raft of her life. Somehow we lift sheep and carry them to higher ground, where they bound away to safety. But the water keeps coming. When a pregnant ewe is stranded on a hillock, William fords the stream to rescue her. I am bursting with happiness.

Then with a great heave Mrs. Gildersleeve let go a long rattling breath that seemed never to end.

At once I was back in the desperate heat of August. Stillness settled over us, into every florid corner, quieting the delicate figurines lining the windowsills, the satiny tongues of exotic plants with impossibly long names, the small naked Buddha, which, Mrs. Gildersleeve had once told me solemnly, needed no clothes. I'd delivered the newspaper one morning and she'd invited me in. The room was heavy with a mysterious fragrance that kindled in me a hunger for that which I did not know—the source of my mother's sadness, for the confidence in Mrs. Gildersleeve's smile, for a story that offered a place for me beyond my own small life.

Zara Raab

## WINTER CALENDARS

Ahead on the narrow road,
a plow pushes a drift aside.
Trees are lately dressed in gauze.
On crusted stones in graveyards
tender hands gloved for the dead
finger time under the moss.
Vised in the ice of winter
is another roll of days.
No giddy, flitting birds
inhabit the snow-stilled woods.
Gnats sleep, so the squirrel and bear
where the buried dead lie.
Seasons of departing sun
bring a sudden darkness, come
barreling under the high beams,
the headlights leading us home,
and an old ache subsides,
and fish dart beneath the ice.

Kelli Russell Agodon

## SONG TO THE QUIET VISITOR

The broken watch was beautiful
just as you, my blue baby, were complete.

I heard your voice opened by doctors,
halls echoed your cry.

Why was hell delivered in color?
In blood and blue body, heartbeats

without breath.  When wind arrived
I thanked the crows that combed through it.

In another room, you wore wires,
numbers, slept in a clean plastic bed, left

hungry. I roamed the hospital.
I was the cloud who could not find

its shadow, could not find the field
who called for it to rain.

Thirsty, my hushed, you slept alone
with your mouth open and I folded

inward, a ripped map without its center,
a motherland of scars.

Angelique Johnston

## WALLPAPER CARS

I hate to forget things:

hydronephrosis
voiding cysto-urethrograms
blue nuclear die testing
bladder cyst
urosepsis
whip-stitched surgical incisions
morphine drip
central line
near acute circular failure.

But some
words turned actions
have no bed
to sleep in
with me.

Everything I or you ever need
lacks a particular linguistic signifier,
exhales without
wallpaper cars and
brightly colored hot-air balloons,
flat, near the edge of the ceiling,
but not quite at the top.

I try to remember a song
about singing on a playground:
lavender's blue, lavender's green…
At what point
do the molecules of creation
and destruction slow their pace
as they find each other's
interlocking stare?

I am here
where time has bent me
on this last day
where babies survive.

Melissa Knox

## MISCARRIAGE AT TEN WEEKS

It plops to the bottom of a coffee cup
With a soft sound, little pillow in blood,
Little paisley still pulsing
I have to warm it
It must stay warm—
Get it
Back inside, where
It can grow,
No arms, no legs, no brain,
But still slick-warm in blood
Still pulsing,
For one long moment.

Cathie Sandstrom

## NO VOYAGING

Breakers all the way to the horizon,
a sea that brooks no voyaging.

Standing on the strand, we look out, wind in our faces.
The others say *I can't imagine how it must feel…*

A gust tears the words from their mouths,
flings them behind us: *to lose a child.*

I put on the clacking wooden coat of a mother
whose son has died, try to make it look natural.

Behind me, the women gather close.
That this has happened to me

means it could happen to them. With whispers
and the laying on of hands, they console each other.

Martha Silano

## THE HARDEST PART ABOUT MOVING

isn't the sorting and packing of paper clips,
the repeat trips to U Haul, the five more loads.
What undoes you isn't recalling, as you pick the last

of the spring greens from your daughter's
secret garden, snap peas gone hippy in the heat,
how the spot where you're standing is where your son

waved goodbye to planes as they passed overhead.
Nor is it sifting through a decade of valentines, watercolors,
progress reports. The most difficult thing is simpler than slinging

clothes into boxes, lugging picture books down two flights of stairs,
the innumerable trips to Goodwill, your Vanagon bursting with crayons,
Groovy Girls, Rainbow Dash. What finally breaks you open begins as a call

from the realtor about a stain no one can remove,
continues as you and your partner head over to where a dresser
has been shielding, for fifteen years, evidence of a baby bottle landing

on its side, spilling out a swath of Similac long dried,
of not exactly having weaned but suddenly childless, your infant
sucking down synthetic milk while medics strap you into an ambulance,

rush you to intake where you announce you're about
to be canonized. Watching as the father of your children kneels,
scrapes, blows away the loosened bits. Him watching you as you scrub.

Both of you rising from your knees to admire the gleaming wood.

Owen Lewis

## URGENCY

A voice, an owl of desperation
I am still blocks away from,
and she cries that she is dying
and she is. My mother, her cousins,
a generation. Her cough hatchets
the dark I race through, the ambulance
blares ahead of me—*Oh friends!*
*Not these sounds!* I lose her, too.
It's dangerous to be alive and lonely.
*Do you come crashing down, you millions?*
And what of the newly painted ceiling,
buckling and cracking, what of the sky,
star points swelling, bursting, extinguishing—

The quoted lines are from Schiller's "Ode to Joy", the lyrics of the final movement of Beethoven's
Ninth Symphony.

## BIRTHDAY MONTH

A moth dive-bombs the candle
the flame sounds, scorching your wings.
            You were my antelope.
            You were my blue heron.
Once I watched
the small pads of your feet
crust over, followed you up
creek.  Once I wound down
into Sabino Canyon alone
then waited for your rattles
to cease, rigid as you drew
your organed length away.

Often, August, I hear your eerie
calls from overlarge tulip trees
though I cannot spy the bird
where you reside.  Leaves slide,
truth elides, oh shadow, oh mother
burning your own effigy
swarming into flame
sucked deep into a waxy under-
world where finally you are mine.

# CLINICAL TRIAL

When the doctor said "Stage IV" that summer,
she thought she'd seen her last daffodil.
She paid a boy to trim the bushes back,
but when he hacked the hosta
to the bare nubs and slashed
the clematis that clung to the trellis,
she felt she too had been cut out.

She slept away the winter, losing weight,
pea-sized lumps multiplying under her skin.
The doctor fought for her, found
a fully human IgG4 monoclonal antibody,
got her in the trial on the day it closed.
In March, she dared to read the seed catalogue,
awoke to tumors shrinking like the snow.
Tiny clumps of grass struggled through the cold ground.
She blessed the daffodils, planted pansies. Daily
she checked the garden, for hosta can be blasted
to their roots and still return.

Lisa Marie Brodsky

# HYSTERECTOMY OF THE ROARING WOMAN

They pinned me down like a struggling butterfly.
Bloated with womanhood still intact,
mornings brought great glaciers over my body;
something was wrong.

I looked at my teenage daughter,
so grateful for her life before the cut that would
remove the great ovarian arms that
once held her so safe.

At least I gave wings to one bird.

Doctors hovered over me like moths
to my lantern. Squelch this light,
they decided. Blow out her
*I Am Woman Hear Me Roar;*
make her sing the blues.

They told me each cell has life,
not just my uterus, but after
the operation I heard the mournful
songs my breasts sang:
*where are my compatriots? Where is
my mothering army?*

Brett Foster

# MY MOTHER AS INADVERTENT OPTIMIST

She managed other flashes of humor, too,
like when she returned from obtaining
lunch for us in the basement café, a meal
of tuna salad on toast and broccoli soup,
and said, with mock surprise, upon seeing
me reclined and of course hooked up
to the IV that held the chemo drugs
and facing four more hours of treatment,
"What, are *you* still here?"

There also arose a certain strain of humor,
something seriously funny, in her
strained efforts, repeatedly made, to make
these long, sedentary days in the cancer center,
where my body absorbed the needed toxins,
somehow impossibly desirable, an experience
full of benefits, as if we had been fortunate,
the lucky recipients of a golden lottery ticket,
which had given us the high privilege of visiting.
"I love coming here with you," she said,
"because it makes you get stuff done."
By the end of the day, with three of the four
infusions completed, and one to go home
with me in a portable pump, she jumped
to her feet and began to collect the water
bottles and newspapers and magazines
that littered our space by then, saying,
"Hey, I'm glad to hear you're really feeling
the side effects this time. That let's you know
clearly that the drugs are really doing
their job. I say, Good for them."

Wendy Vardaman

## from POSTCARDS FROM THE MUSEUM OF CHILDHOOD

#12

my neighbor learns to mow
her yard. she waves at us
from done, from *see*, from learn
new things in retirement, sweeps
her arm in front of her & smiles.
it's a little shorter than her husband
would have liked, a little shorn.
he's been gone three months.
I miss his *hello, beautiful day,*
daily slow walk around the block
when I think of him, which
isn't often. she seems ok.

Carley Moore

## CODE

It's the way of cells to divide.

In the YouTube videos
      I see my own long divisions.

This nuclear split makes two daughters.

The new cells rub up against each other,
      share a wall, and vibrate with proximity.

If the kernel of life is to separate and iterate,
      then why do I cling to wrecks?

These ossified hulls.
      This cleaving.
            Barnacle.  Bivalve.

I'll feel along the shared wall of the one who left.

There's a code there,
      now just to crack it.

Rachel Edmonds

## LEAVING

Blame is elusive,
pins in haystacks, broken
doors that swing both ways,
squeaky hinges grinding. Perpetual
dark, forgotten, for one brilliant
day. Fractured eggshells
sprinkled on black earth,
keeps the slugs away, the edges
too sharp, pierce the flesh.

The therapist said I had to
mean it; if I left.
Not as a battle strategy
to elicit a counter response
of remorse. Words dipped
in honey, dangling the moon
at my doorstep, begging
the sun to come out, the light
to filter the dark.

The only one on the doorstep
now is me, weighted down
by barefoot children. Tattered
indecision makes fools of us. I made you
do it, for me, or you made me.
We'll never know.

Jamie Stern

# DIDN'T WE JUST

wasn't it just summer
weren't we just sitting
on concrete floors
near failing stores
rattled by the wind

weren't we just dancing
didn't we just wed
worried that our mothers
would clash with their mothers
and others

wondering what would change
with our exchange
of rings
sure that everyone
alive would stay that way

weren't they all just dancing
weren't they all just here
when did they start to go
with no goodbye

when did we need to remember
to see them
how well can we see them
that summer

baking on the beach
when tan was in
and we were in
everything

weren't we just hip to hip
lip to lip
as if we always would
and everyone always could
be reached by phone

wasn't it just summer
didn't we just kiss
weren't we just sitting
on a concrete floor
wanting more
as if we always would
always could

## FORM IN BLUE

Blue tinged, but not clinical.
Not can't-get-out-of-bed
bad. Not work stoppage.
Just simple; sitting on the empty
overturned hard plastic
bin that used to hold the cat
litter, in my bathrobe, drinking
coffee and smoking cigarettes
on-the-front-stoop blue.

Like that. Like, functional but
not glass half full. Like thirst.
Like depleted uranium. Like still
deadly but not in its original form or
not meeting its original purpose.

Like dry skin and tight skull
jaw clenching, teeth grinding
like she-needs-to-get-laid blue,
like it's hard to forget you
those vows you lied through.

M. Joy Rose

## CHANGE

You cannot bend the branch of fate.
Once it's grasped, it's bound to break,
And whittled into tools of pain
We stab at change, to change again.

Jennifer Martelli

## DROWNED GIRL AND DOOMED BOY

I'm awake by the blue light of the tv muted so as not to rouse my husband.  A drowned girl
       crawls from the set and lands, hands and knees
(with a grunt, I guess) on a doomed boy's rug.

I wonder if we can love something and not want to drag it down. I pick a strand
       of my own hair off my tongue and examine:  it's still black and my sight
is good enough to read the subtitles, good enough to see its sheen in the flickering blue—

the worst light to try to sleep in.  The body in rest believes it's under water, the ring in
       the eye dilates and constricts, teased, alert, even when closed.
I wonder if we still love something if we stop looking at it.

I can hear the glass man pull the unredeemable bottles from our blue bin and smash them on
       the sidewalk, leave the slivers for me to sweep once they stop reflecting
the streetlights and moon and stars, like hundreds of eyes looking up.

Lori Lamothe

# THE AGORAPHOBIC'S DREAM

A few moments scatter across the beach.
They flame up from our footprints
like trick birthday candles or dusk's
resurrected dogs. Foaming shore,
solid sky distance, closeness of your voice,
of wind waving grass, umbrellas tilting.

Here light bounces off everything tangible—
shells and broken glass, sand and horizon,
screech of gulls, the sea. If I close my eyes
the glare diamonding water is still
blinding. Fire haunts my skin, my hair,
settles onto words I've collected
in my bucket of silence. Reality's
sticky, a grit between my teeth,
the kind of glitter that won't wash off.

I don't know if I'm a coward or not.
I don't know what you'd say if I asked
because I don't ask. Either way
I'm fluent in the language of fear,
can shutter my mind against angles
in a single bound, wrap moth wings in wool
for safekeeping. Don't get me wrong.
Tomorrow I'll walk tightropes with strings of hearts
tied round my ankles, write your name in circles
across the blue, blue air.

Carla Carlson

# EXPANSION

I turn towards the mirror, off-put,
saying to my eyes, what dear?
Take heart—I've stuffed rosebuds
in drawers. We'll carry them to the city
in a drawstring. We'll fall into place
like jewels in the valley, like pointillism
at sunset.  I shall be flooded with
floral aroma. Perhaps the moon's full.
Last night, when I felt like a cow,
breasts hanging over my husband,
his eyes were there, and there
was nothing I could do to stop
this body from offering.

Lois Marie Harrod

## HUMMING TOO

Instead of singing, she decided to hum,
that burr on lips, mumble of mucous.

Her fantasy: to be the thrumming
at the inner drone, that self-sufficient.

At dusk, a thundercloud rumbled the mountain,
wet there but not here. Coming.

Coming too early. Fumbling too late,
Light run of thumbs. Any part she chose.

Strumming the bass in her hand,
glum string shivering in the heat.

She remembered a man
who made instruments of bumbling things—

toilet plungers, strapless bras,
spinning jennies

porcelain spoons, bent spittoons
saffron plums descending.

She liked to hear him change.

## WHATEVER WAS ALIVE

She knelt in the attic closet holding a spider made of synthetic fiber, bending legs, and battery-operated eyes that had stopped working years ago. Even without glowing red irises, the spider frightened her with its fierce look and gnarled body. She remembered hanging it in the dining room last Halloween and her son looking the other way when they had eaten dinner together. "How long do we have to keep it there?" he had asked when he cleared his plate. "We'll know," she had replied. Now, she threw it out of the closet onto a pile of boxes on the rug in the attic's main room.

She had started cleaning out the house after her husband left. At first, she tore through bookshelves and kitchen cabinets, ridding herself of all the junk she had tolerated when he was still around. She had cried while packing old books and CDs into paper bags and had felt elated when he carried the bags to his mother's truck and one of them ripped, old books spilling onto the lawn. When that work ended a few weeks earlier, she had made her way into the attic to wrestle with things hidden behind doors only he used to open.

The spider was the last of it. She hauled the vacuum cleaner from the basement up the stairs and plugged it into the wall next to an old dollhouse. She watched with satisfaction as dust and small pieces of insulation flew up the nozzle into some dark place inside, keeping an eye out for nails or wood scraps or pieces of insulation too large for the machine.

That's when she saw it.

At first she thought it might be an old rag so she started to pick it up with her hand, but she stopped when she saw it move. Just a small movement, something pulsing on the wooden floor. She stared for a moment, fascinated. This wasn't an old rag. This was a beating heart, something terrible and alive. She turned off the vacuum and climbed down the attic stairs to get a cup. She didn't think about how clean the kitchen was, no more junk, only dishes and teapots and ceramic bowls she knew she wanted to keep. Back in the attic she didn't think about the dollhouse with its dining-room table knocked over and windows painted shut. She didn't think about anything except that tiny heart exposed on the wooden floor.

She crawled back into the closet and gently placed the cup over the beating heart. Now, she needed a piece of cardboard. One hand pressing down the cup, she used her other hand to tear the lid off an old box and slide it into place. Immediately, whatever she had trapped inside began to stir, fast. Her hand firm on the cup, she felt its body flutter, struggling against the plastic. Holding her breath, she lifted the cardboard and crawled as steadily as she could out of the closet into the attic's main room, where light from the windows spilled over piles to keep and piles to throw away forever. She inched through the piles, down the attic stairs, out of the house, and as far into the open air as she could in that small moment of her changing life.

A tall pine stood in the yard. She looked at its trunk, its branches, the needles that had fallen to the ground, the roots digging more deeply than she could imagine. Still feeling whatever was alive banging beneath her fingers, she extended her arms towards the tree and closed her eyes, trying to gather something from the darkness. Then, she opened her eyes and watched herself lift the cup from the cardboard, watched the body arc into the world, fall, then rest against the earth, still except for its pulsing heart. She turned and retraced her steps back into the house whose closets and cabinets also pulsed, and she knew that when she looked out the window later that day she would see nothing but dirt and needles and sky.

Dana Bowman

## DERAILMENT

Under the bed:
a cat-furred journal,
the other sock,
Thomas the train, derailed

Next to my bed:
A bible,
a glass of vodka,
both half full.

I have been emptying my life
into a chipped glass
every night.

One morning, so thirsty,
I tipped the glass
and watched it shatter.

And I found:
my boys, my marriage, the journal,
and derailment,
 a gift.

Patricia Brody

## RIGHT TO CHOOSE

Underfoot I will throw on some schmatta
but understress I turn to whiskey, or I whine, or other

medication.  Lately I prefer meditation.
Make it all go away. Only the moment

matters, let these thoughts go.
I invited someone to take over. I loved when he climbed
                                                    my tree

bound my hair to my own low bow. Oh his
thumb. *You choose* I begged, and he

did make a salad, hand me a fork, and let me
                    make my own way home in the dark.
The white branches hung heavy at dusk.

I came to the edge of his park.
No kid played at that hour.  Why else
                    do we who choose, choose

children.  Yes we cradle, coax them through the night
(you have to *shush*, not make a move, make sure

they don't die in their sleep) but the grand prix, to focus

your high beam on someone else! not Your Self:  Lay thee down
under unbalanced boulder, waiting for the fault,

dear Portia, in our
winking stars.

## ON THE ROAD

Sometimes the words
step out of the poem
and you can see all the way
to the horizon of meaning,
the images transparent
as sky in winter—
the air fading to a color
you can't name.

That's when you notice
the house aglow
at the edge of seeing,
its row of windowpanes
flickering uncertainties
that tempt you
to set out on a journey
that might change your life,
might not.

Claudia Van Gerven

## COURAGE

Think of all the brave and stupid things you've done:

waking to the heart-sick lyrics of
unwed birds

leaning—without thought—on a tilted planet
just drinking coffee and brushing your teeth

The poles, they say, are about to do si do, metal
filings, the fillings in your teeth begin to twitch

True north as fickle as the lottery—
still you buy your ticket

You start your car. The road meanders to the same old
place, the trees explode with pollen.

You might float up the stairwell full of
God like Catherine of Sienna

or just watch shadows harden along the carved leg
of the wing-backed chair

Your mirror is full of foreign faces.  You're trying
to keep up. You know where this is headed:

Tonight again you will curl in a field of flowered
sheets, arrange yourself in that familiar curve

and remember how to forgive

Wendy Vardaman

## from POSTCARDS FROM THE MUSEUM OF CHILDHOOD

#24

we grope our way forward. worry
about fall & fall off this flat.
there is black ice at the border
of fine & we keep sliding. there
is fog. you can't see your
feet let alone. you hope
to find your way back some.
not to *happy* which never. but
to *well.* to *well enough.* to get
there you have to understand
what it is to be *there.* you have to
be there. you have to *are* there.
& you must twist every word
in half/break/crack this wor(l)d
open between your teeth. pick
at its meet. it is tense at the *edge*
*of okay.* you may have to go on alone.

#25

there were things to tell you but
physical therapy. cleaning the fridge.
cat litter. there were meals to make
& messages. if you stop folding
clothes. stop alphabetizing
cabinets & childhood. but there
still isn't enough. there were idioms
to learn. culture. I did not want to
say the things I wanted to say
in the language I had to say them.
but *mother* is the only tongue I know
& when the calendar says *jump,*
I say where. I say when.

# CONTRIBUTORS' NOTES

**Kelli Russell Agodon** is the author of six books, most recently, *Hourglass Museum* (Finalist for the Washington State Book Award & shortlisted for the Julie Suk Poetry Prize) & *The Daily Poet: Day-By-Day Prompts For Your Writing Practice.* She is also the cofounder of Two Sylvias Press where she's an editor and book cover designer. www.agodon.com / www.twosylviaspress.com. She blogs at www.ofkells.blogspot.com.

**E.J. Antonio** is a recipient of fellowships from the Hurston/Wright Foundation, the Cave Canem Foundation and the New York Foundation for the Arts. She is the author of two chapbooks, *Every Child Knows,* (Premier Poets Chapbook Series 2007) and *Solstice,* (Red Glass Books, 2013), and a CD, *Rituals in the marrow: Recipe for a jam session.* www.ejantoniobluez.net.

**Robyn Art** is the author of *The Stunt Double in Winter* (Dusie 2007) which was a Finalist for the 2005 Sawtooth Poetry Prize as well as the 2005 Kore Press First Book Award. Her chapbook *Farmer, Antagonist* won the 2015 Burnside Review Chapbook contest and will be published in Spring 2016. Her newer manuscript, *Amplitude, Awe,* was recently selected as a Finalist for the 2014 Burnside Review Book Award.

**Felice Aull** is a mom, grandmother, and recently widowed. She began writing poetry in her 60s. She has a chapbook, *The Music Behind Me.* Recent poems are in *Off the Coast, Connecticut River Review,* and *Riverbabble.* She was full-time faculty at New York University School of Medicine and is now adjunct in the Department of Medicine's Division of Medical Humanities. www.feliceaull.com.

**Lisa Badner's** poems have appeared in online and print magazines including, *Mudlark, TriQuarterly, Fourteen Hills, Ping Pong, Poetica, New World Writing, PANK* and *Vine Leaves Literary Journal.* Lisa lives in Brooklyn with her partner and son and she can usually be found riding a bicycle.

**Tess Barry** was shortlisted for the 2015 Manchester Poetry Prize (England). Twice a finalist for North American Review's James Hearst Poetry Prize and Aesthetica's (England) Poetry Award, she was shortlisted for the 2014 Bridport Poetry Prize (England). Her poems recently appear in Mudfish and at MMU's website. She teaches literature and creative writing at Robert Morris University in Pittsburgh. http://www.manchesterwritingcompetition.co.uk/2015-Manchester-Writing-Competition-short-lists.pdf.

**Sarah W. Bartlett** midwifes stories that evoke and celebrate voice, growth and change among women. Since January 2010, she has led *writinginsideVT* within Vermont's sole women's prison. Poet and essayist, Sarah has contributed to respected academic and literary journals, and highly-acclaimed anthologies. She celebrates what is true within each of us as compass and guide. www.sarahwbartlett.com.

**Deborah Batterman** is the author of *Shoes Hair Nails* (short stories) and *Because my name is mother* (essays). She is a Pushcart nominee and took 3rd place in the Women's National Book Association 2012 Short Fiction Contest. Her blog has evolved into a collaboration with her daughter. She can't say she invented the word, but a 'diablog' it is.

**Margo Berdeshevsky's** newest poetry manuscript was finalist for the 2015 National Poetry Series. Her published collections are *Between Soul & Stone,* and *But a Passage in Wilderness* (Sheep Meadow Press.) Her *Beautiful Soon Enough* (University of Alabama Press) received Fiction Collective Two's

Innovative Fiction Award. Other honors include the Robert H. Winner Award from the Poetry Society of America. http://margoberdeshevsky.blogspot.com.

**Pam Bernard**, a poet, painter, editor, and adjunct professor, received her MFA in Creative Writing from the Graduate Program for Writers at Warren Wilson College, and BA from Harvard University. Her awards include an NEA, two Massachusetts Cultural Council Fellowships, and the Grolier Prize. Her most recent book is a verse novel entitled *Esther*, published by CavanKerry Press.

**Emily R. Blumenfeld** is a writing facilitator in the area of the transformative and therapeutic uses of language. She has published both literary and scholarly writing, and her writing and work center on themes of social justice, women's equality, and the well being of mothers and children.

**Dana Bowman** is a wife, a mother, a teacher, a writer, and a runner, simultaneously. This is only possible because her family donates loads of material. She has been published in numerous magazines, and is the proud author at Momsieblog.com. Her book, *Bottled: How to Survive Early Recovery*, published by Central Recovery Press, is now available. One day, she hopes to master the skill of making sure all dessert apportionment is *completely* equal.

**Maria Brandt** has published short work in several literary magazines. Her longer work includes *New York Plays* (Heartland Plays), *All the Words* (Evening Street Press), and Pam Mills' posthumous memoir *Kamastone* (Jaded Ibis Productions), which Maria edited and introduced. Maria teaches at Monroe Community College and is a founding member of Straw Mat Writers. She lives with her son William. www.mariafbrandt.com.

**Lisa Marie Brodsky** is the author of *We Nod Our Dark Heads* (Parallel Press 2008) and *Motherlung*, (Salmon Poetry 2014) which was recognized by the Wisconsin Library Association as a 2015 Outstanding Achievement in Poetry. Lisa served on the Southeast Wisconsin Festival of Books as a panelist on healing and writing and is on faculty at AllWriters' Workplace & Workshop. http://www.lisamariebrodsky.com.

**Jennifer Brooke**, a writer/filmmaker, studied poetry with Billy Collins. Publications include: *East Hampton Star, RFD Magazine, The Sun, Hartskill Review, Rubbertop Review, TSR-The Southampton Review*. She co-directed *Out Late*, (released by First Run Features), and the soon-to-be released *Legs: a big issue in a small town*. Jennifer is married to her film partner, Beatrice Alda, and they have 5 kids.

**Patricia Brody's** first full length collection *Dangerous to Know (*Salmon, 2013) followed a chapbook, *American Desire,* (Finishing Line New Women's Voices Award,2009). Poems appeared in *Levure Litteraire, Paris Review, Psychoanalytic Perspectives, BigCityLit, Poetry Daily*. She is featured poet in Fall 2015 *The Hardy Review*. Patricia and artist/photographer Tom Kostro raised three (now "adult" but still-growing) children one block from the Hudson River. Currently teaching Seeking Your Voice: Women Writing Today, recently of the Barnard College Center for Research on Women.

**Carla Carlson** holds an MFA from Sarah Lawrence College's writing program. Her poems have been published in various journals such as *Prelude Magazine, The Westchester Review, Columbia, Catch And Release, Chronogram Magazine*, and others. Her debut chapbook, *Love And Oranges*, was published by Finishing Line Press in September 2015.

**Judith Waller Carroll** is author of *The Consolation of Roses*, winner of the 2015 Poetry Prize from Astounding Beauty Ruffian Press, and *Walking in Early September* (Finishing Line Press, 2012). Her work appears in numerous journals and anthologies, including *River of Earth and Sky: Poems for the Twenty-first Century* (Blue Light Press, 2015), and was nominated for Best of the Net.

New to the role of grandmother, **Deb Casey** values process and overlapping fields of imagery in her art and writing. The recipient of an NEA in Poetry, she has published her poems in *Zyzzyva, Calyx, Ploughshares, Prairie Schooner, Chicago Review* and other magazines and anthologies. Her chapbook *As-Is, Several Sisters*, was published recently by Finishing Line Press.

**Fay Chiang** is a poet and visual artist who believes culture is a spiritual and psychological weapon used for the empowerment of people and communities. Working at Project Reach, a youth center for young people at risk in Chinatown/Lower East Side, she is also a member of the artists collective Zero Capital; the Orchard Street Advocacy and Wellness Center, which supports people affected by HIV/AIDS, cancer and other chronic illnesses and voluntarily teaches art and creative writing workshops to incarcerated youth at Rikers Island. Battling her 8th bout of breast cancers, she is working on her memoir. *Seven Continents Nine Lives* (Bowery Books) is her most recent collection of poetry. And she is the mentor to her Tribal Kids and the mother of the inimitable Xian.

**Laura A. Ciraolo** was born in New York City and has lived and worked there as long as she can remember. Her poems have appeared in *The Cortland Review, The New York Quarterly, Mom Egg Review*, and *Agenda* among others. She was a finalist for The Bordighera Poetry Prize 2013, and published a cookbook entitled *Slop and Ugly Onions: A Family Cookbook Memoir*.

**Patrice Boyer Claeys** holds a certificate in poetry from The Writer's Studio at the University of Chicago. She enjoys Monday nights as a member of Serious Play, Alice George's poetry workshop in Evanston, Illinois. Her work has appeared in *The Found Poetry Review, The Avocet, Blue Heron Review, Ardor*, and the *Mom Egg Review*, where she served as a reader for Volume 14.

**Marion Cohen's** latest poetry book is *Lights I Have Loved* and her latest memoir is *Still the End: Memoir of a Nursing Home Wife*. Her books total 27, including *What I'm Wearing Today*, a forthcoming poetry chapbook about thrift shopping. She teaches math and writing at Arcadia University and her book, *Crossing the Equal Sign*, is about her passion for math. Her website is www.marioncohen.net.

A proud mother of two, **Nadia Colburn** lives in Cambridge, MA. Her work has been widely published in *The New Yorker, American Poetry Review, LARB, Southwest Review*, and elsewhere. A founding editor at *Anchor Magazine: where spirituality and social justice meet*, Nadia teaches online and in person creative writing workshops that bring together the head and the heart. See more at www.nadiacolburn.com.

**Barbara Crooker's** poems have appeared in journals and anthologies including *The Bedford Introduction to Literature* and *Good Poems American Places*. She has six full-length books of poetry, including *Small Rain* (Purple Flag Press, 2014) and *Barbara Crooker: Selected Poems* (FutureCycle Press, 2015), and her work has appeared on *The Writer's Almanac* and Ted Kooser's *American Life in Poetry*. www.barbaracrooker.com.

**Lorraine Currelley,** Poet, Writer, Storyteller, Executive Director for Poets Network & Exchange, Inc., Collagist, and Mental Health Counselor. She's widely anthologized. The recipient of the NYPL Arts for A Lifetime Grant, Bronx Council for the Arts Seniors Partnering with the Arts Citywide Residency, BinderCon Scholar Grants, a WWBPS Community Service Award and TWH Residencies. A Board Member at Pen To Mind Books & Child Development Concepts, Inc. and Blind Beggar Press, a Bronx Book Fair Committee Member and a Writing for Peace, Inc. Advisor. Featured in DoveTales *Nature, An International Journal of the Arts*, Poets & Writers Cross Cultural reading and AWP Spotlight. https//poetsnetworkandexchange.wordpress.com.

Metro Detroit writer **Jenifer DeBellis** is *Pink Panther Magazine's* editor and a former fellow for the Meadow Brook Writing Project. JDB is an adjunct creative writing instructor and a workshop facilitator for Oakland University's Meadow Brook Writing Camps. Her poetry and prose appear in the *Good Men Project, Literary Orphans, Sliver of Stone, Solstice Lit Mag*, and other fine journals.

**Sally Deskins** is an artist, writer and scholar focusing on the perspectives of women in art. Her work has been exhibited and published widely. She is founding editor/curator of Les Femmes Folles, an organization dedicated to women in art. She is also a happy mama to May and Henry who collaborate, cheer-on and inspire her work. sallydeskins.tumblr.com.

**Kelly Dolejsi** is a stay-at-home mother/climbing instructor with an MFA from Emerson College. Her work has been published in *Mothers Always Write, Trickster, Santa Fe Literary Review, Bitter Oleander*, and *Phantasmagoria*, and is forthcoming in *Denver Quarterly*.

**Carol Dorf's** poetry has been published in *Mom Egg Review, Spillway, Sin Fronteras, Antiphon, Composite, About Place, The Journal of Humanistic Mathematics, Scientific American, Maintenant, OVS, Best of Indie Lit New England*, and elsewhere. She is poetry editor of *Talking Writing* (talkingwriting.com) and teaches mathematics at Berkeley High School.

**Katherine Durham Oldmixon's** recent poems appear in *Borderlands, Solstice, The Normal School, Bellevue Review, Cactus Heart*, and in her chapbook *Water Signs* (New Women's Voices 67, Finishing Line Press). Katherine co-directs the Poetry at Round Top festival, is a senior poetry editor for *Tupelo Quarterly*, and professor and chair of English at Huston-Tillotson University in Austin, TX. katherinedurhamoldmixon.com.

**Rachel Edmonds** is mother to two children and currently finishing an honours degree in English and Creative Writing at Dalhousie University in Halifax, N.S. She was awarded first prize in the Clare Murray Fooshee Poetry Contest in 2015. Her poems have appeared in *Fathom*, Dal's undergraduate journal and *Understorey Magazine*.

**Joanne Esser** writes poetry and nonfiction in Minneapolis, Minnesota. She has also been a teacher of young children for over thirty years. She earned an MFA in Creative Writing from Hamline University and published a chapbook of her poems, *I Have Always Wanted Lightning*, in 2012. Her work appears in *Water-Stone Review, The Sow's Ear Poetry Review, Third Wednesday* and *Young Ravens*, among other magazines.

**Sarah Evans** is an Oregon writer and editor of the online magazine *Salem Is* (www.salemis.org). Her work has appeared in *The Quotable, Bluestem, Brevity's* nonfiction blog and *River Teeth's Beautiful Things* blog. She is a graduate of the MFA in writing program at Pacific University.

**Kate Falvey's** work appears widely in journals and anthologies. She has published two chapbooks, *What the Sea Washes Up* (Dancing Girl Press) and *Morning Constitutional in Sunhat and Bolero* (Green Fuse Poetic Arts). Her book, *The Language of Little Girls*, is forthcoming this summer from David Robert Books. She edits the *2 Bridges Review* (www.2bridgesreview.org), published through City Tech/CUNY, where she teaches, and is on the board of the *Bellevue Literary Review*.

**Ann Fisher-Wirth** is the author of four books of poems, most recently *Dream Cabinet* and *Carta Marina* (Wings Press, 2012 and 2009), and coeditor of *The Ecopoetry Anthology* (Trinity UP, 2013, 2014). A fellow of the Black Earth Institute, recipient of two senior Fulbrights, past-president of ASLE, she has received numerous awards for her poetry. She teaches at the University of Mississippi.

**Brett Foster** authored two poetry collections, *The Garbage Eater* (Triquarterly Books/Northwestern UP, 2011) and *Fall Run Road*, which was awarded the Open Chapbook Prize. His writing has appeared in *AGNI, Boston Review, IMAGE, Kenyon Review, Pleiades, Poetry Daily, Raritan, Seattle Review, Southwest Review*, and *Yale Review*.

**Cindy Frenkel's** poetry has been in *The MacGuffin, The Alembic,* and *Renaissance City*—her prose in *Vanity Fair* and *The New York Observer*, where she was a columnist. She wrote/edited the museum magazine *DIA* and co-authored *100 Essential Books for Jewish Readers*. Frenkel's essay about being a Writer-in-Residence with InsideOut Literary Arts Project appears in *To Light a Fire.*

**Nancy Gerber** is a writer and psychoanalyst whose work has been published in *Mom Egg Review, Adanna Literary Journal, Menda City Review*, and other publications. Her most recent book, *Fire and Ice: Poetry and Prose* (Arseya, 2014), was nominated for a Gradiva Award in poetry.

**Sarah Ghoshal's** work can be found in journals such as *Arsenic Lobster, Red Savina Review, Reunion: The Dallas Review* and many others. She has two chapbooks, *Changing the Grid* (Finishing Line Press, 2015) and *The Pine Tree Experiment* (Lucky Bastard Press, 2015) and was recently nominated for Best of the Net. She is currently working on a collection highlighting the first year of parenthood.

**Therese Gilardi** is a poet, essayist and novelist whose work has appeared in *Literary Mama, Punchnel's, Mom Egg Review, The Dirty Napkin* and numerous other publications. Therese is the author of the novels *Narvla's Celtic New Year* and *Matching Wits With Venus*. Therese adores Irish pub music, blue cameos and chocolate cannoli. http://theresegilardi.com.

**Heather Haldeman** lives in Pasadena, California. She has been married to her husband, Hank, for thirty-seven years and has three grown children. Her work has been published in *The Christian Science Monitor, Chicken Soup for the Soul, From Freckles to Wrinkles, Grandmother Earth, Mom Egg Review,* and numerous online journals. She has received first, second and third prizes for her essays. Currently, she is working on a memoir about growing up in wealth and ruin in Los Angeles during the Mad Men era.

**Lois Marie Harrod's** 13th and 14th poetry collections *Fragments from the Biography of Nemesis* and the chapbook *How Marlene Mae Longs for Truth* appeared in 2013. Her poems and stories have appeared in journals and online ezines from *American Poetry Review* to *Zone 3*. Read more work on www.loismarieharrod.org.

**J.P. Howard** is a Cave Canem graduate fellow. She is the author of *Say/Mirror*, a debut poetry collection published by The Operating System (2015) and a chaplet, *bury your love poems here* (Belladonna Collaborative*, 2015). JP curates and nurtures Women Writers in Bloom Poetry Salon (WWBPS), a forum offering women writers a venue to create new work monthly.

**Alison Condie Jaenicke** teaches writing at Penn State University, where she also serves as Assistant Director of Creative Writing. She studied at the University of Virginia (BA/MA, English). Her essays, stories, and poems have appeared in such publications as *Superstition Review; Gargoyle Magazine; Isthmus; Brain, Child;* and *Literary Mama*. Samples of her work can be found at her website: http://alisoncjaenicke.weebly.com/.

**Angelique Johnston** teaches writing and literature at Monroe Community College in Rochester, NY, where she lives with her supportive husband and two teenage daughters. She's passionate about gender, social equality, and the recovery of trauma and grief, and feels rather fortunate to be surrounded by an encouraging circle of women writers. Her creative nonfiction has been published in *The Genesee Valley Parent* and www.ImperfectParent.com.

**Donna Katzin** is Executive Director of Shared Interest, social investment fund that promotes equitable development in Southern Africa. She also coordinates Tipitapa Partners, which works with communities of organized women in Nicaragua, and serves on the board of the Center for Community Change in the US. She is the proud mother of Sari and Daniel Altschuler, and author of *With These Hands*, a collection of her poems and photographs, available from Shared Interest (Sandra@sharedinterest.org) that focuses on South Africans on the front lines of their country's struggle for economic justice.

**Sarah Kennedy** will graduate from Penn State University's M.A. in humanities program in May 2016 and holds an undergraduate degree from Elizabethtown College. She plans to teach at the university level and facilitate therapeutic writing workshops.

**Dr. Juanita Kirton** earned MFA from Goddard College, 2015. She is a member of Women Who Write and Women Reading Aloud. She directs the QuillEssence Writing Collective and is currently the poetry editor for *Clock House Literary Magazine*.

**Melissa Knox's** recent poems have appeared in *NonBinary Review* and *The Feminist Wire*. Essays have appeared in *Brain, Child* and *Gravel*. She teaches American and English literature and culture at the University of Duisburg-Essen. She has written extensively on Oscar Wilde and other nineteenth-century English writers. She loves the work of Sharon Olds, Billy Collins and Charles Simic.

**Sandra Kohler's** third collection of poems, *Improbable Music*, (Word Press) appeared in May, 2011. Earlier collections are *The Country of Women* (Calyx, 1995) and *The Ceremonies of Longing*, winner of the 2002 Associated Writing Programs Award Series in Poetry (University of Pittsburgh Press, 2003). Her poems have appeared in journals, including *The New Republic, The Beloit Poetry Journal, Prairie Schooner*, and many others over the past 35 years.

**Lori Lamothe** is the author of two poetry collections, *Trace Elements* and *Happily*, as well as several chapbooks, mostly recently *Ouija in Suburbia* with dancing girl press. New work appears in *Painted Bride Quarterly, The Literary Review, Verse Daily* and *failbetter*, which nominated her for a Pushcart prize.

**Carol Levin's** collections include full volumes, *Confident Music Would Fly Us to Paradise*, MoonPath Press 2014 and *Stunned By the Velocity*, Pecan Grove Press 2012. Chapbooks, *Red Rooms and Others*, Pecan Grove 2009 and *Sea Lions Sing Scat*, Finishing Line Press 2007. Levin's an Editorial Assistant at the journal *Crab Creek Review* and teaches The Breathing Lab/Alexander Technique in Seattle. www.the-breathing-lab.com.

**Owen Lewis** is the author of *Best Man, Sometimes Full of Daylight*, and *March in San Miguel*. He has received awards from *The Mississippi Review, Connecticut River Review*, London School of Jewish Studies, Ver Poets (UK), and Amherst Writers and Artists Press. He is a physician and a professor at Columbia University.

**Tsaurah Litzky** is a widely published poet, writer of fiction, erotica, plays, memoir and commentary. Her full length poetry collections are *Baby On The Water* and *Cleaning The Duck*. Her sixteenth poetry chapbook, *My Shackles Melt*, is due out this summer. She lives on the Brooklyn waterfront and sees the Statue of Liberty from her kitchen window.

**Charlotte Mandel's** ninth book of poetry, *Through a Garden Gate* with color photographs by Vincent Covello, is published by David Robert Books. Her awards include winner of the New Jersey Poets Prize and two fellowships in poetry from New Jersey State Council on the Arts. Her critical essays include a series on the role of cinema in the life and work of H.D. Visit her at charlottemandel.com.

**Jennifer Martelli's** chapbook, *Apostrophe*, was published in 2011. Most recently, her poetry has appeared in *Wherewithal, Up the Staircase Quarterly*, and *Rogue Agent*. Her reviews have appeared in *Glint, Arsenic Lobster*, and *Drunken Boat*. She is a recipient of the Massachusetts Cultural Council Grant in Poetry, a Pushcart and Best of the Net nominee and is an associate editor for *The Compassion Project*. She lives in Marblehead, Massachusetts with her family. www.jennifermartelli.com.

**Jessica Martinez** spent most of her life in various European countries before moving to Greater Hartford, Connecticut, with her young family in 2014. She started writing at age 9 and she was an active writer as a student. Then life had other plans and she only just rediscovered her passion. One of her latest poems appeared in *Literary Mama*.

**Ann E. Michael's** poetry has appeared in print and online, and has been featured in several anthologies with parenting themes, although her topics range from chickens to philosophy, sometimes simultaneously. Her book *Water-Rites* is available through Brick Road Poetry Press. She blogs at www. annemichael.wordpress.com.

**Tracy Mishkin** is a call center veteran with a PhD and an MFA student in Creative Writing at Butler University. Her chapbook, *I Almost Didn't Make It to McDonald's*, was published by Finishing Line Press in 2014. Her work has appeared recently in *Hartskill Review, Little Patuxent Review*, and *The Quotable*. https://tracymishkin.wordpress.com.

*Dinner with Emerson*, **Wendy Mnookin's** most recent book, is out this spring from Tiger Bark Press. Her other books are *The Moon Makes Its Own Plea, What He Took, To Get Here*, and *Guenever Speaks*. She lives with her husband in Newton, Massachusetts, where they raised their three children. You can find out more at wendymnookin.com.

**Carley Moore** is a poet, novelist, and essayist. Her work has appeared or is forthcoming in *The American Poetry Review, Brainchild, The Brooklyn Rail, The Establishment, GUTS, The Journal of Popular Culture, Mutha, Public Books*, and *Tinderbox*. She co-curates the reading series Dynaco Studio in Brooklyn and is currently working on a semi-autobiographical novel called *Gold Star*. Twitter: carleymoore2 Website: carleymoorewrites.com.

**Eve Packer** is a Bronx-born, poet/performer, actress, mom & grandmom--3 books, (from Fly By Night Press), the most recent: *new nails* (2011). 5 poetry/jazz CD's with saxophonist Noah Howard, also Stephanie Stone, and with Daniel Carter & others. Most recent: eve packer: *ny woman, poetry/jazz highlights* (2015). Lives downtown, swims daily.

**Laura Sloan Patterson** is an English professor at Seton Hill University in western Pennsylvania and the author of *Stirring the Pot: The Kitchen and Domesticity in the Fiction of Southern Women*. Her poetry has appeared or is forthcoming in *The Written Wardrobe: An Online Anthology, Pittsburgh Poetry Review, Rust + Moth*, and *Not One of Us*.

**Theta Pavis** is a poet and journalist. Her work has been published in numerous journals, including *The Journal of New Jersey Poets, The Red Wheelbarrow* and *Mom Egg Review*. As the Director of Student Media at New Jersey City University, she works with first-generation college students. Her poetry was recently performed as part of the Emotive Fruition project in Brooklyn and Manhattan.

**Amy Pence** authored the poetry collections *Armor, Amour* (Ninebark Press, 2012) and *The Decadent Lovely* (Main Street Rag, 2010). Pence has published in *The Antioch Review, The Oxford American* and *Juked*, among others. Her fiction and non-fiction have appeared in *WSQ, The Rumpus, Poets & Writers* and *The Writer's Chronicle*. She teaches in Atlanta, Georgia, and lives in Carrollton. www.amypence.com.

**Puma Perl** is a performer, producer, and a widely published poet/writer. She's the author of two chapbooks, *Belinda and Her Friends* and *Ruby True*, and two full-length collections, *knuckle tattoos* and *Retrograde*. As Puma Perl and Friends, she performs with some of NYC's best musicians and merges poetry with rock n roll. She is a regular contributor to The Villager. http://pumaperl.blogspot.com.

**Andrea Potos** is the author of six poetry collections including *An Ink Like Early Twilight* (Salmon Poetry), *We Lit the Lamps Ourselves* (Salmon Poetry) and *Yaya's Cloth* (Iris Press). A short-short collection entitled *Coffee in Greece* is forthcoming from Anchor & Plume Press this spring. Her work appears widely in print and online.

**Zara Raab's** books are *Fracas & Asylum* and *Swimming the Eel* (David Robert Books); her chapbooks (Finishing Line) are *The Book of Gretel*, and *Rumpelstiltskin*, a finalist for the Dana Award. Poems and reviews appear in *Verse Daily, River Styx, Arts & Letters, Crab Orchard Review, Raven Chronicles,* and *The Dark Horse*. She lives in Massachusetts. Visit her at www.zararaab.com.

**Margaret Rapp** As a first wave feminist, I try to give voice to the shared vulnerability of all women while still focusing on the differences in our experiences and oppressions. Whether it is the result of racism, class, age, disability, religion, ethnicity, status as a mother, single or married - I try to honor women in all our diversity and complexity.

**Gwen North Reiss** has published poems in *Rhino, Truck, Connecticut Review, Dogwood,* and other literary magazines. Her poem, "Illuminated," was the winner of the 2012 Rachel Wetzsteon Prize at the 92nd Street Y's Unterberg Poetry Center. She is a writer and communications consultant.

**Martha Joy Rose** is a scholar, mother, and founder of the band Housewives On Prozac. Teaming up with other artists, academics, and activists, Joy pioneered the Mamapalooza Festival in 2002 and then opened the first-ever Museum of Motherhood in 2011. She is currently teaching at Manhattan College and has written for Sage Press, Demeter Press, and assorted literary journals.

**Margaret Rozga** has published three books of poetry, *Justice Freedom Herbs, Though I Haven't Been to Baghdad*, and *200 Nights and One Day*. She has been a resident at Ragdale and at the Sitka Center for Arts and Ecology and was awarded a 2014 Creative and Performing Artists and Writers Fellowship by the American Antiquarian Society.

**Kassie Rubico** is an essayist currently working on a memoir. Her work has appeared in *Guide to Kulcher Creative Journal,* the anthology, *River Muse, Tales of Lowell and the Merrimack Valley, Toska Literary Magazine* and *Pithead Chapel*. She received an MFA in Creative Nonfiction at Pine Manor College and teaches writing at Northern Essex Community College.

A military brat, **Cathie Sandstrom** has published in *Ploughshares, Runes, Lyric, Solo, Comstock Review, Cider Press Review, Malpais Review, ART/LIFE, Ekphrasis, New Plains Review* and *Wide Awake: Poets of Los Angeles and Beyond* among others. A poem with essay appears in *Master Class: The Poetry Mystique*. Her poem "You, Again" is in the artists' book collection, Getty Museum, Los Angeles.

**Amy Sawyer** is a poet residing in Washington, DC with her husband, two young children, and one sweet old dog. She studied philosophy at Clemson University and earned her MFA at Converse College. Her work has been published and is forthcoming in *Stand Magazine, Mud Season Review, South Carolina Review*, and *Conclave Journal*. She manages the website allpoetryisprayer.com.

**Marian Kaplun Shapiro**, a previous contributor to *MER*, is the author of a professional book, *Second Childhood* (Norton, 1988), a poetry book, *Players In The Dream, Dreamers In The Play* (Plain View Press, 2007) and two chapbooks: *Your Third Wish*, (Finishing Line, 2007); and *The End Of The World, Announced On Wednesday* (Pudding House, 2007). A Quaker and a psychologist, her poetry often embeds the topics of peace and violence by addressing one within the context of the other. A resident of Lexington, she was five times named Senior Poet Laureate of Massachusetts. She was nominated for the Pushcart Prize in 2012.

**Martha Silano** is the author of *Reckless Lovely, The Little Office of the Immaculate Conception, Blue Positive, What the Truth Tastes Like,* and, with Kelli Russell Agodon, *The Daily Poet: Day-By-Day Prompts For Your Writing Practice*. Martha edits *Crab Creek Review* and teaches at Bellevue College.

**Ana C. H. Silva** lives in NYC with her husband and 8-year-old daughters. Her poetry has been published in *Podium, Mom Egg Review, the nth position, Snow Monkey, Anemone Sidecar, Chronogram,* and *Stepaway Magazine*. She won the inaugural Rachel Wetzsteon Memorial Poetry Prize at the 92nd St. Y Unterberg Poetry Center.

**Meghan Smith** has been writing poetry for the past four years. Her work has appeared in *Mom Egg Review* and *Blast Furnace*. She teaches English in Groton, Massachusetts where she lives with her husband, spit-fired daughter, and squishable baby boy.

**Maura Snell** is co-founder and poetry editor at The Tishman Review and teaches poetry writing and critique to incarcerated teen girls. Her works have appeared both online and in print in various journals, most recently in *Brain, Child Magazine*. She lives outside Boston with her family and her two rescue mutts.

**Jamie Stern's** poetry collection, *Chasing Steam*, was published in January 2013. Her poem, "Posted," appears in an anthology published in 2015 by Lamar University Press, *Pushing the Envelope: Epistolary Poems*. An attorney in NYC, Jamie is the co-publisher of five poetry anthologies in honor of Marie Ponsot, *Still Against War I-V*, and a member of the board of Poets House.

**Kelli Stevens Kane** is a Cave Canem Fellow and an August Wilson Center Fellow based in Pittsburgh, PA. She's studied at VONA, Hurston/Wright, and Callaloo. Her recent work is published or forthcoming in *North American Review, Little Patuxent Review, Split This Rock,* and *Delaware Poetry Review*. For more information visit kellistevenskane.com.

Poet and essayist **Christine Stewart-Nuñez** is the author of *Untrussed* (forthcoming 2016 from the University of New Mexico Press), *Snow, Salt, Honey* (Red Dragonfly Press 2012), *Keeping Them Alive* (WordTech Editions, 2011), and *Postcard on Parchment* (ABZ Press 2008). Her piece "An Archeology of Secrets" was a Notable Essay in *Best American Essays 2012*. She is an Associate Professor in the English Department at South Dakota State University. http://christinestewartnunez.wordpress.com.

**L.J. Sysko's** work has appeared in *Best New Poets 2013, Amazon's Day One, Ploughshares, Rattle,* and other journals. She holds an MFA in poetry and is English department chair at Tower Hill School in Wilmington, Delaware. Contact her at ljsysko@gmail.com, find her on Twitter @ ljsyskopoet, or stop by ljsysko.com.

**Claudia Van Gerven's** poems have been published in numerous journals including *Prairie Schooner, Georgetown Review* and *Calyx*. Her work has appeared in numerous anthologies and has been nominated for the Pushcart Prize. Her chapbook, *The Ends of Sunbonnet Sue*, won the Angel Fish Press Poetry Prize. Her most recent chapbook is *Bearing Witness*, Finishing Line Press (2014).

**Wendy Vardaman** (wendyvardaman.com) is the author of *Reliquary of Debt* (LitFest Press 2015) and *Obstructed View*, co-editor of *Local Ground(s)--Midwest Poetics and Echolocations, Poets Map Madison,* and founding co-editor of Cowfeather Press (cowfeatherpress.org). She served as poet laureate of Madison, Wisconsin, 2012-2015. Connect with her on Twitter @wendylvardaman.

**Cindy Veach's** poems have appeared most recently in *Michigan Quarterly Review, The Journal, Valparaiso Poetry Review, Poet Lore, North American Review, The Human,* and *Crab Creek Review*. She is a volunteer for Mass Poetry (masspoetry.org) and makes her living managing fundraising programs for nonprofit organizations. She lives in Manchester, MA.

**Susan Vespoli** lives in Phoenix where she teaches English at a downtown community college, rides her bike along the canals, and walks her 3-legged dog Jack. Her poetry and prose have been published online and in various print anthologies and journals.

**Kimberly Weikert** earned her Master's degree at St. Bonaventure University where she primarily studied Victorian poetry and prose. Currently, she spends most of her writing time composing grants and other technical documents, although she still takes time out to occasionally script a poem or two. She is director of the Twin Tiers Writers workshop, a group in western New York that meets weekly to turn prompts into prose. She lives at home with her husband and two teenage children and a peculiar array of domestic animals.

**Hilde Weisert's** poetry collection *The Scheme of Things* was published in 2015 by David Robert Books. Her poems have appeared in such magazines as *Ms, Calyx, Prairie Schooner, Cincinnati Review,* and the *Cortland Review*. Recent readings include several with the Berkshire Festival of Women Writers. She lives in Sandisfield, MA and Chapel Hill, NC. Visit her at www.hildeweisert.com.

**Elisabeth Weiss** teaches at Salem State University in Massachusetts. She's taught poetry in preschools, prisons and nursing homes as well as to the intellectually disabled. Her poems have appeared in many journals including *Crazyhorse, the Birmingham Poetry Review,* and the *Paterson Literary Review*. A chapbook, *The Caretaker's Lament*, was published by Finishing Line Press. Visit her website at www.elisabethaweiss.com.

**John Wojtowicz** grew up working on his family's azalea and rhododendron nursery in the backwoods of South Jersey. He is currently employed as a social worker and takes every opportunity to combine this work with his passion for wilderness. Besides poetry, he likes bonfire, boots, beer, and bluegrass. He was most recently published in *Stoneboat, Five2one, Naugatuck River Review,* and *El Portal*.

**Megan Wynne** is a multimedia artist based in Chesapeake, Virginia. Her work addresses issues of interdependence and intimacy, with a focus on the subject of motherhood. Megan holds a BFA in Sculpture from Pratt Institute, and a MFA in New Genres from San Francisco Art Institute. Her work has been exhibited internationally, including The Lab, Stephanie Roper Gallery, and The Virginia Museum of Contemporary Art.

# MOM EGG REVIEW

**Mom Egg Review Issues Available**

| | | |
|---|---|---|
| Vol. 14 "Change" | 2016 | Paper, 128 pp. $18 |
| Vol. 13 "Compassionate Action" | 2015 | Paper, 154 pp. $18 |
| Vol. 12 | 2014 | Paper, 150 pp. $18 |
| Vol. 11 "Mother Tongue" | 2013 | Paper, 125 pp. $18 |
| Vol. 10 "The Body" | 2012 | Paper, 120 pp. $18 |
| Vol. 9 | 2011 | Paper, 120 pp. $18 |
| Vol. 8 "Lessons" | 2010 | Paper, 120 pp. $18 |
| Vol. 7 | 2009 | Paper, 124 pp. $18 |

*Plus US shipping $3.50 for the first book, $1.00 for each additional book.

Email info@themomegg.com for info about discounts for quantity purchases and for classroom use, or for out-of-country shipping.

## Subscribe to MER

*US shipping is free for subscription copies!*

One year  $18
Two years $36

Mail your order with a check to

**Mom Egg Review**
**Half-Shell Press**
**PO Box 9037**
**Bardonia, NY 10954**

MOM EGG REVIEW
*Literature & Art*

Contact:  info@themomegg.com

Order on the web at
**www.momeggreview.com** (Click "Shop")